WHERE TO
FIND THE BEST
SOUL FOOD,
BLUES, AND JAZZ
IN THE
SOUTHEAST

To my wife Elizabeth

All information is accurate as of press time. However, prices can change and establishments can close or go downhill; therefore all information herein should be regarded as a guidemark and is not guaranteed by the author or publisher. In the interests of keeping this book accurate, we would appreciate hearing from you regarding any errors or omissions. If you have noteworthy experiences in the establishments listed herein or if we have excluded good places, please write. All contributions will be appreciated and acknowledged. Address your letters to:
Ron Rudison c/o Elliott & Clark Publishing,
P. O. Box 21038, Washington, DC 20009-0538.

Edited by Elizabeth Brown Lockman
Designed by Gibson Parsons Design
Printed and bound in the U. S. A. by Bang Printing

Any inquiries should be directed to Elliott & Clark Publishing,
P. O. Box 21038, Washington, DC 20009-0538
telephone (202) 387-9805

WHERE TO FIND THE BEST
SOUL FOOD,
BLUES, AND JAZZ IN THE SOUTHEAST

By Ron Rudison

ELLIOTT & CLARK PUBLISHING
Washington, D.C.

TABLE OF CONTENTS

4

5

✗ *Indicates soul-food restaurant*

FOREWORD

The soul-food restaurant occupies a very special place in African American culture. Traditionally, the term "soul food" brings to mind a meal consisting of an entree such as chitterlings with side dishes of greens—either collard, mustard, or turnip—rice and gravy, candied yams, and corn bread. The term "soul-food restaurant" embodies a cultural institution, a place where African Americans have traditionally come together after church, after work, or even after an evening out. The best soul-food restaurants have always been anchors of their respective communities, and for this reason, the establishments in this book have been selected as much for their cultural ambience as for the quality of their food and the selection on their menus. Accordingly, traditional soul-food restaurants as well as those specializing in southern and Creole cuisine, barbecue, and fish are included.

African slaves brought many skills with them on their unwilling journey to America. Their knowledge of woodworking and metallurgy served their masters well during slavery. After they gained their freedom, these same skills enabled them to dominate the trades as artisans. Slaves also came to America with the syncopated rhythms and melodies of Africa. They merged these with the European adaptations of the plantation owners and created a new music, a music that evolved from field chants to spirituals to ragtime and ultimately to blues, jazz, and gospel. African American cuisine evolved in a similar fashion. The slaves brought to the Americas a knowledge of spices and herbaceous roots, as well as recipes for transforming even the gamiest meats into culinary works of art. Add this to the lush vegetables, fruits, and grains of the Native Americans and the livestock introduced by planters and plantation owners, and you have the basic scenario for the evolution of soul food.

In effect, the two living conditions encountered by slaves in field quarters and in the "big house" resulted in the development of two separate, but related cuisines. The vast majority of slaves lived in field quarters and were more often than not given inferior cuts of meat: from the hog, entrails, feet, ears, and so on; from the chicken, wings, feet, gizzards, liver, and the like. As a means of economic necessity and survival, slave cooks adapted these coarse ingredients to sustain the field hands.

Meanwhile, slave cooks in the "big house" invariably prepared the choicest cuts of meat. Smothered pork chops and steaks, beef stew, and fried, smothered, or baked chicken utilized the best ingredients money could buy. Ironically, the slave cook's magic with bitter greens made them irresistible even to the residents of the plantation proper. When these plantation owners entertained guests from other parts of the country and abroad, their visitors must have been struck by the fresh, robust, and exciting cuisine produced by the slave cooks. Imagine also their surprise when they heard the strange, syncopated new music emanating from the slave quarters.

Nowhere was this scene more often repeated than in the Mississippi Delta. The Mississippi Delta is a region along the border of Arkansas that ranges as far south as Vicksburg to just south of Memphis. To travel along Mississippi's Highway 61 is to retrace the history of one form of the blues in America. Vicksburg, Rolling Fork, Greenville, Indianola, Cleveland, Clarksdale, and Tunica all parallel the highway that snakes along the border like its neighbor, the Mississippi River. At the turn of the 20th century, these Delta towns were the birthplace of many of America's blues legends. Son House, Mississippi John Hurt, Robert Johnson, Albert King, B. B. King, Memphis Minnie, McKinley Morganfield (Muddy Waters), Charlie Patton, and Bukka White are but a few from a very long list. Even before them, musicians were roaming the Delta, putting to music the hard conditions of life in the cotton fields that had their origins in slavery. This was a fertile environment for a young composer, W. C. Handy, to add form to the music, put it on paper, and share it with the rest of the United States and the world.

Even before W. C. Handy was plying the Delta in search of the blues, Scott Joplin was refining another of America's original musical forms, ragtime. His syncopated piano style and numerous ragtime compositions earned him distinction as the king of rag. The emergence of blues and ragtime during the first decade of the 1900s captivated the entire country.

Also in the first decade of the century, a young cornet player in New Orleans named Buddy Bolden was taking ragtime and blues in a different direction. His improvisations on the cornet were mirrored by most of the young musicians of the city. Pianist Jelly Roll Morton and cornetist Joe "King" Oliver left New Orleans and took the music to Chicago, where, during the second decade of the century, jazz found a fertile environment and exploded across America. It also spread rapidly throughout Europe when Mobile, Alabama, native James Reese Europe took his 369th Infantry Division Band to Europe during World War I and brought African American music to a world stage.

Listen to Albert Collins's "Soul Food," James Arnold's "Red Beans and Rice," or Lou Rawls singing about "red beans and rice and candied yams," and you will get an idea about the relationship between the food and the music. As Charlie Davis of C. Davis Bar-B-Q in Houston puts it, "the barbecue and the blues just go together." So does jazz and Creole cuisine, according to Nina Buck of the chic Palm Court Jazz Cafe in New Orleans. Musicians and entertainers have always sought out soul-food restaurants during their travels. In many ways, the music and the food are both defining elements of the people.

During the early 1940s and through the early 1950s, a period of American history when segregation was the rule, African American travel guides focused on three basic questions: Where can I stay? Where can I eat? and Where can I go for entertainment? One such guide, The Negro Green Book, published in 1952, attempted to answer those questions in an ambitious project that covered cities across the country. One of the most interesting lists in this book cited the major African American thoroughfares in each city.

In a historical context, this list of famous streets chronicles the best of African American culture from the Harlem Renaissance of the 1920s through the mid-1960s. It also recalls what existed before single-family home-owners were displaced and their land was put to use for public projects such as interstate freeways. Huge, multi-family complexes replaced many private dwellings, and more affluent African Americans moved to the suburbs, setting the stage for the collapse of the inner cities in general, these streets in particular. Many of the great theaters, clubs, and soul-food restaurants of the 1940s and 1950s also have been lost as a result. Some that have survived are highlighted in this book.

The international appeal of blues and jazz is well documented. In fact, blues and jazz artists historically have found their most appreciative audiences in Europe, Asia, and South America. The appeal of soul-food restaurants likewise crosses all cultural lines. Whether they are in Memphis, New Orleans, or Little Rock, their clientele typically represents all segments of their respective communities. The establishments included here are the best of the best.

Note to the reader: The listed price range for soul-food restaurants includes an entree, two or three side dishes, corn bread or rolls, and a drink such as lemonade, iced tea, or soda:

> Very Modest = less than $7
> Modest = $7-$10
> Moderate = $10-$15

While the soul-food restaurants in this book are relatively stable, clubs come and go, and the demands in the marketplace can influence changes in format. Be sure to call before your visit.

ATLANTA, GEORGIA

Atlanta is the cultural and financial center of the African American community in the Southeast and, many contend, the entire nation. Here, African American entrepreneurship is more than just a concept, it is a historical fact.

Atlanta has one of the largest populations of African American millionaires per capita of any city in the world. Alonzo F. Herndon was Atlanta's first. Born a slave in 1858, he overcame those shackles and, in freedom, found an entrepreneurial niche as a barber. He opened several barber shops, invested in real estate, and became so successful that he was able to found the Atlanta Life Insurance Company, one of the nation's most prosperous African American financial concerns. His son, Norris, carried on that tradition. Both he and his father were also pioneering African American philanthropists.

The median standard of living for African American residents ranks among the country's highest. This broad economic base, plus a large number of registered minority voters, has translated into a broad political base. Political luminaries such as Julian Bond, Maynard Jackson, Mary Young-Cummings, and Andrew Young help chart the course of the city today. The latter, the nation's first African American ambassador to the United Nations, also was a key member of the committee that secured Atlanta as the host city for the 1996 Summer Olympics.

Atlanta's current cadre of African American leadership is impressive, but there were many who paved the way before them. W. E. B. Du Bois, a man who fired political debate and cultural awareness throughout the African American populace, taught at Atlanta University during the late 1890s. Atlanta native the Reverend Dr. Martin Luther King, Jr., captured the imagination and hearts of the world while leading the Civil Rights movement in the late 1960s. Morehouse, Spelman, and Morris Brown colleges, along with Clark Atlanta University, have helped generations of African Americans develop their full potential. Notable graduates include Dr. King, Lerone Bennett, Jr., and many other men and women who have left a profound and continuing legacy for the entire country.

Atlanta's entertainment options are equally impressive, making it a must see on any trip through the Southeast, be it for business or pleasure.

MUSIC

BLIND WILLIE'S

Location: 828 N. Highland Ave.
Telephone: (404) 873-BLUE
Clientele: Young/Mature Adult
Format: Blues
Calendar: Live Entertainment Nightly
Cover/Minimum: Yes/No
Dress: Casual/Classy

Comments: Named after Atlanta's most renowned blues star, "Blind Willie" McTell, Blind Willie's looks and feels like everything a blues club should be. The building dates back to the 1920s or 1930s, and the club is a cozy rectangular room with high ceilings and low lights. The bricks and floor are original. Most of the seating is snug up against the stage, with a few tables located across from the sit-down bar in the rear of the room; all seats give an unobstructed view of the performers. Eric King and his partner, Roger Gregory, founded the club in February 1986. King had long hosted his own blues show on WRFG-FM (89.3) radio, and he knew what Atlantans wanted. Although Blind Willie's started out on a shoestring budget, it had a good nucleus of local blues artists who were starving for exposure, and the club has since become the city's foremost venue for launching the careers of its native talents. Some of the most popular local acts that have been featured here include Luther "Houserocker" Johnson (regularly appearing with the Shadows), Sandra Hall, and Lotsa Poppa. (Poppa often toured with legendary R & B crooners Jerry Butler, Sam Cooke, and Jackie Wilson during the 1960s and was a regular feature at Atlanta's famed Royal Peacock club.) The partners also brought in national touring acts, mostly friends they had met at events such as the annual New Orleans Jazz & Heritage Blues Festival. Atlantans have really taken to this establishment, and rightfully so. It's a place where you can hear the New Orleans-flavored blues of the Roulettes on one evening, the Texas-style blues of Johnny Copeland on another, and the Delta influences of the legendary David "Honeyboy" Edwards on a third. King, who considers himself a blues buff almost from birth, and blues sideman Gregory have long nurtured a love affair with this American art form, and as a result, they have given Atlanta one of the most important blues venues in the southeastern United States.

DANTE'S DOWN THE HATCH

Location: 3380 Peachtree Rd. NE/60 Upper Alabama St. (Underground Atlanta)

Telephone: (404) 266-1600/577-1800

Clientele: Young/Mature Adult

Format: Jazz

Calendar: Live Entertainment Nightly

Cover/Minimum: Yes/No

Dress: Classy

Comments: Dante Stephensen always has been a man of entrepreneurial vision, from the days of his childhood lemonade stands and newspaper routes. His tour in the Navy as a member of the Underwater Demolition Team and later as a founding member of the Navy's elite SEAL Team, and his service in Vietnam forged in him the discipline and toughness to stay true to that vision. Paul F. Mitchell, a longtime fixture in Atlanta's jazz scene, recalls meeting Dante Stephensen when he performed at Atlanta's Playboy Club in the mid-1960s. Stephensen told Mitchell that he was going to build a premier jazz supper club with Mitchell as his featured artist. In 1970, Stephensen founded Dante's Down the Hatch in Underground Atlanta. True to his word, the Paul F. Mitchell Trio has been the feature act from the very beginning, and their music is superb. The club in Underground Atlanta lasted until 1981 when the Underground Atlanta Corporation closed. Stephensen built another, larger version of the club in Buckhead in 1981. His original Down the Hatch was reopened in 1989 with the revival of Underground Atlanta. Each club has a combination you are not likely to find at any other: fine dining and elegant jazz, both showcased in a setting that gives the illusion of an 18th-century sailing vessel tied to the docks of a Mediterranean sea village. When you walk across the "moat" into the club, you'll see live crocodiles, all securely lodged in a confined area below, of course! I counted six at the Buckhead location. Seated at a table on the second floor, I had the sensation of being in a low-slung crow's nest with the band only a few feet away. Everyone's been here, from former Presidents Jimmy Carter and George Bush to entertainment giants Charlton Heston and Gladys Knight. This is simply a must stop when visiting Atlanta!

FATT MATT'S

Location: 1811 Piedmont Ave. NE
Telephone: (404) 607-1622
Clientele: Young/Mature Adult
Format: Blues
Calendar: Live Entertainment Nightly
Cover/Minimum: No/No
Dress: Casual

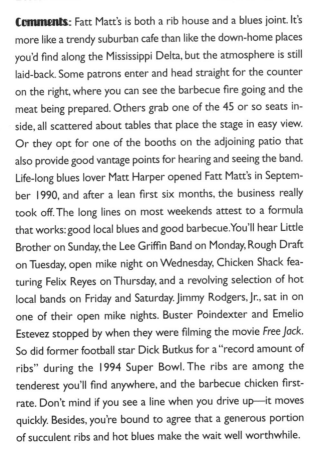

Comments: Fatt Matt's is both a rib house and a blues joint. It's more like a trendy suburban cafe than like the down-home places you'd find along the Mississippi Delta, but the atmosphere is still laid-back. Some patrons enter and head straight for the counter on the right, where you can see the barbecue fire going and the meat being prepared. Others grab one of the 45 or so seats inside, all scattered about tables that place the stage in easy view. Or they opt for one of the booths on the adjoining patio that also provide good vantage points for hearing and seeing the band. Life-long blues lover Matt Harper opened Fatt Matt's in September 1990, and after a lean first six months, the business really took off. The long lines on most weekends attest to a formula that works: good local blues and good barbecue. You'll hear Little Brother on Sunday, the Lee Griffin Band on Monday, Rough Draft on Tuesday, open mike night on Wednesday, Chicken Shack featuring Felix Reyes on Thursday, and a revolving selection of hot local bands on Friday and Saturday. Jimmy Rodgers, Jr., sat in on one of their open mike nights. Buster Poindexter and Emelio Estevez stopped by when they were filming the movie *Free Jack*. So did former football star Dick Butkus for a "record amount of ribs" during the 1994 Super Bowl. The ribs are among the tenderest you'll find anywhere, and the barbecue chicken first-rate. Don't mind if you see a line when you drive up—it moves quickly. Besides, you're bound to agree that a generous portion of succulent ribs and hot blues make the wait well worthwhile.

JUST JAZZ

Location: 595 Piedmont Rd. NE
Telephone: (404) 897-1555
Clientele: Young/Mature Adult
Format: Jazz
Calendar: Live Entertainment Wed.–Sun.
Cover/Minimum: Yes/No
Dress: Classy

Comments: Just Jazz has developed quite a following since it exploded on Atlanta's jazz scene in 1991. Proprietor J. O. Wyatt, a former Fulton County commissioner, felt that if Atlanta was truly to emerge as an international destination, the city needed a top-flight jazz club that regularly featured some of America's touring jazz legends. Just Jazz fits the bill very nicely. A noticeably international clientele throngs to the club's doors. What's all the fuss about? The answer, simply, is outstanding jazz. If you come in for a performance by the house band, what you get is the fabulous Johnny O'Neal Trio. O'Neal, formerly of the Jazz Messengers, is accompanied by Little Jimmy Scott's nephew, Kermit Walker, on drums, and Berkeley School of Music graduate Ramon Pooser on bass. On other evenings, you can expect touring performers such as Kenny Burrel, George Duke, Milt Jackson, and Cassandra Wilson. Don't be surprised if a celebrated artist just drops by unannounced and sits in on a set. Jazz pianist Joe Sample, Stevie Wonder, and the siren of blues and jazz, Nancy Wilson, all have. The theme is musical throughout, from the timbale drum that serves as a ticket holder at the door to the grand-piano-shaped bar inside. The decor is sleek black and white. The club seats about 200, but can expand to 300 when they open their private party room to accommodate the largest shows. Just Jazz's success has not gone unnoticed. It was proclaimed best jazz club in the city by *Atlanta Magazine* for 1992 and 1993. A reader's poll in the underground newspaper *Creative Loafing* voted it best in 1993 as well. An equally impressive accolade came from the July 1993 issue of *Details* magazine, where the club was cited among the "top 300 nights out from Halifax to Honolulu." Just Jazz more than lives up to the billing it has received and should be counted as one of your top entertainment options for rounding out a visit to Atlanta.

LA CAROUSEL

Location: 830 Martin Luther King, Jr., Blvd.

Telephone: (404) 577-3150

Clientele: Mature Adult

Format: Jazz

Calendar: Live Entertainment Fri.–Sat.

Cover/Minimum: No/Yes (1 Drink)

Dress: Classy

Comments: La Carousel, located in the historic Paschal's Hotel, remains a beautiful testament to the vision of the hotel's founders, James and Robert Paschal. As you enter from the restaurant, a platform encased in glass allows you to view the entire club. Take a seat on one of the circular bar's comfortable stools, partially covered with soft white leather, and notice the feel of something intangible. Perhaps it's an aura of power, of momentous action lying at the edge of something yet unspoken. After all, this is a room where Atlantans have come to discuss matters of import for decades. Listen to the conversations around the bar, and you'll find men and women waxing poetic on subjects ranging from the latest campaign plan to urban renewal. Overhead is a colorful canopy of the kind you would find on a merry-go-round. Two antique wooden carousel horses prance in one corner. Murals depict pensive circus clowns. Many jazz and R & B legends have played here. Jazz pianist Ramsey Lewis performed for the club's grand opening in 1959, and Ray Charles, Lou Rawls, and Count Basie were among the long list of renowned entertainers who followed. In recent years, the club has not booked national acts, preferring instead to showcase local jazz artists. The Herman Mitchell Trio is the latest to headline in what is still one of the coziest and most attractive jazz rooms in town.

OTTO'S

Location: 265 E. Paces Ferry Rd. NE
Telephone: (404) 233-1133
Clientele: Young/Mature Adult
Format: Jazz/Top 40
Calendar: Live Entertainment Wed.–Sat.
Cover/Minimum: No/No
Dress: Classy

Comments: Otto's is an upscale nightclub in trendy Buckhead. They started out as a somewhat yuppie bar and sandwich shop in 1986, but they have since expanded their format to include live jazz and eliminated the sandwiches to concentrate on providing live entertainment to a clientele consisting mostly of young Atlanta professionals. The first floor features a piano bar in a room dominated by plush seats, polished mahogany, and brass railings. Upstairs, the action is much less sedate, with the house band, Uptown Express, belting out traditional jazz standards as well as top 40 hits. While Otto's has the ambience of a private club, it's actually a neighborhood bar, albeit an elegant one. Their gourmet pizza adds yet another nice touch. This attractive establishment has often played host to visiting celebrities, from crooner Michael Bolton to rock star Elton John. If you want to spend an evening grooving to the Uptown Express or just lounging in luxurious leather, stop by.

THE ROYAL PEACOCK

Location: 186 Auburn Ave. NE
Telephone: (404) 880-0745
Clientele: Young Adult
Format: Reggae/Calypso
Calendar: Live Entertainment Varies; Dancing Fri.–Sat.
Cover/Minimum: Yes/No
Dress: Casual

Comments: In the 1950s and 1960s, The Royal Peacock was the place to go in downtown Atlanta for African American entertainment. It was a stylish showcase for top R & B, blues, and jazz acts—if you could play The Royal Peacock, your next stop had to be the fabled Apollo in New York City. Mention the Peacock to longtime residents of Atlanta, and the stories start to flow. Dorothy Clements, owner of the Auburn Avenue Rib Shack, recalls legendary performances by artists such as jazz vocalists Cab Calloway, Nat King Cole, and Nina Simone. Doug Berry, maintenance technician for the Chit-Chat Restaurant & Lounge, says that he used to slip into the Peacock as a teenager and take in great R & B acts such as Bobby "Blue" Bland, Clarence Carter, Sam Cooke, Johnnie Taylor, and Jackie Wilson. The Royal Peacock has gone through a number of iterations since those storied years. The current managers, Berhane Hagos and Angelo Gebrehiwet, have implemented a reggae and calypso format that is popular among international students at the various universities in the city. Well aware of The Royal Peacock's important place in Atlanta's history, Gebrehiwet hopes to restore the club to its former splendor and bring back some of the 1950s and 1960s acts who played here in its heyday.

TEDDY'S LIVE ENTERTAINMENT

Location: 121 Central Ave. (Underground Atlanta)
Telephone: (404) 653-9999
Clientele: Young / Mature Adult
Format: Jazz / Blues / R & B / Gospel
Calendar: Live Entertainment Nightly
Cover/Minimum: Yes / No
Dress: Classy

Comments: Teddy's Live is a beautiful new supper club show-casing top jazz, blues, and R & B acts. The room is elegant and expansive, seating 325 comfortably. Dining tables are woven throughout the club, almost caressing the raised stage and dance floor. One dining area to the right of the stage is elevated about eight inches and encircled by brass rails. Picture windows over-look Kenny's Alley and the Coca Cola Plaza, and a skylight tops the stage. Terraces and a full-service patio offer open-air dining when the weather entices. A varied menu with specialties such as prime rib, baked rainbow trout, pasta primavera served with alfredo sauce, and chicken or shrimp adds to the allure; so does the Sunday Champagne Brunch. The specially designed sound system of speakers and amplifiers is fully integrated throughout the club so that performers need only to plug their instruments into outlets at the rear of the stage to prepare for a show. Teddy's Live reflects proprietor Teddy Astin's impressive resume in en-tertainment. It goes one better on the celebrity photos found in many clubs; framed glass displays of gold record albums are placed throughout the dining room, each presented to Astin as the national director of marketing and promotions for Warner Brother's Records. Astin started out in the warehouse at Warner Brother's in the early 1970s and worked his way up the corpo-rate ladder. When he retired from the company in August 1993, he and his wife Joyce opened Teddy's Live. As they have already featured Jean Carn, Michael Henderson, Joe Sample, and Noel Pointer, I would say they are off to an impressive start. This is an entertainment supper club to place high on your itinerary when visiting Atlanta. Make reservations for one of their superb shows, or just stop by for an outstanding dinner, served daily from 4:00 P.M.

DINING

ALECK'S BARBECUE HEAVEN

Location: 783 Martin Luther King, Jr., Blvd.
Telephone: (404) 525-2062
Proprietor: Pamela Alexander
Dress: Casual
Menu: Barbecue/Soul Food
Price: Modest
Hours: Mon.–Wed.: 11:00 A.M.–
10:00 P.M.; Thurs.: 11:00 A.M.–
11:00 P.M.; Fri.–Sat.: 11:00 A.M.–2:00 A.M.

Comments: Ernest Alexander built this rib house in the early 1950s, and it has been one of the great Southern barbecue restaurants ever since. Alexander's daughter Pamela has maintained the family tradition. Recently elected to Atlanta's city council, she has lots of help keeping the restaurant going as you'll often find a third generation of Alexanders tending the grill. The service is excellent, the ribs and veggies are superb, and the flavors and aromas remind me of summertime family reunions. I often ate here when I was a student in the 1960s, and it will always remain one of my favorites.

19

AUBURN AVENUE RIB SHACK

Location: 302 Auburn Ave. NE
Telephone: (404) 523-8315
Proprietor: Dorothy Clements
Dress: Casual
Menu: Barbecue/Soul Food
Price: Modest
Hours: Tues.–Thurs.: 11:30 A.M.–4:00 P.M.;
Fri.: 11:30 A.M.–9:00 P.M.; Sat.: 12:00 P.M.–9:00 P.M.

Comments: This historic rib house was founded by Allen J. and Mary C. Taylor in 1962. Allen Taylor opened his first restaurant, a popular barbecue shop on Bell Street, in the early 1950s. According to his daughter Dorothy Clements, this experience, a partnership, cemented his love affair with the restaurant business. Taylor operated several other small sandwich shops in Atlanta's West End during the late 1950s and early 1960s, and when he got the chance to acquire a property on Atlanta's still-booming Auburn Avenue in 1962, he leapt at it. That was a time when, as Clements recalls, you could walk down Auburn Avenue on Sundays and see African Americans dressed to the hilt. A lifelong member of the historic Ebeneezer Baptist Church, she would spend the morning in church and then ask permission to watch the elaborate parades put on by the Elks and Prince Hall Masons. The Reverend William Holmes Borders and the Reverend Martin Luther King, Sr., would patrol the avenue, tending to the faithful. King Senior's entire family would stop by the restaurant for barbecue. Clements took over the restaurant in 1982, fulfilling a promise she made to her late father. Her mother, Mary Taylor, still makes the secret, tomato-based barbecue sauce from scratch. This establishment still occupies a special place in the hearts of most Atlantans. The succulent barbecue ribs are the most-requested dish on the menu. Many also favor the collard greens and macaroni and cheese. The restaurant is tiny by any standards, with seating for 12, so most patrons stop by for take-out orders. The Auburn Avenue Rib Shack offers an opportunity to relive some of Atlanta's rich history, savor outstanding ribs, and experience the down-home hospitality of the Taylor-Clements family, and for me that's a winning combination.

THE BEAUTIFUL RESTAURANT

Location: 2260 Cascade Rd./397 Auburn Ave.

Telephone: (404) 223-0080/752-5931

Proprietor: The Perfect Church

Dress: Casual/Classy

Menu: Soul Food/Southern

Price: Very Modest

Hours: Daily: 7:00 A.M.–8:30 P.M.

Comments: The Beautiful Restaurant is one of Atlanta's finest for soul food and Southern cuisine. The Perfect Church, a Holiness congregation, opened their initial restaurant in 1979. They have owned five restaurants over the years, but have settled on two, their original Beautiful Restaurant at the Cascade location in southwest Atlanta and one on the city's historic Auburn Avenue, adjacent to the Ebeneezer Baptist Church and the Martin Luther King, Jr., Memorial. The church started their first eating establishment because they wanted a place where congregation members could get fresh vegetables cooked in all-natural oils, without pork. It was an immediate success. The Beautiful Restaurants are perfect examples of economic empowerment, and their delicious meals are a fantastic value. Many Atlanta natives come here for the restaurant's vegetable platter (three veggies, cornbread, and a beverage for $3.19!), but I couldn't resist the baked Cornish hen, rice pilaf, and collard greens. I had my entree at the Auburn Avenue restaurant and saved room for dessert at the Cascade location. There Mrs. Lenora Reese, general manager, surprised me with three different desserts: peach cobbler, apple cobbler, and banana pudding. They were all delicious beyond words. Other items you'll find on the menus of both restaurants include braised short ribs, T-bone steaks, chicken-flavored rice, squash, and green beans. The restaurant on Auburn has seating for about 50, and its decor is somewhat spartan compared to the Cascade location, with its numerous potted plants and meticulously landscaped lawn. The latter is my favorite for sit-down dining. A display case houses fresh, homemade apple and carrot juice along with garden salads. The decor is alive with hues of gold, orange, and white. The Cascade location seats 88. Both restaurants offer excellent dining options.

DEACON BURTON'S SOUL FOOD

Location: 1029 Edgewood Ave. NE
Telephone: (404) 658-9452
Proprietor: Lenn Storey
Dress: Casual/Classy
Menu: Soul Food
Price: Very Modest
Hours: Mon.–Fri.: 7:00 A.M.–4:00 P.M.

Comments: Deacon Burton's Soul Food is a cozy, no-frills eatery tucked away in a white brick building across from the Inman Park Metro Station. When you walk through the serving lines, you can choose among several trays heaped with fried chicken, fried fish, lima beans, corn bread, and banana pudding. Several cooks behind the counter busily keep the trays filled or tend to the old burners in back. Around noon, the restaurant quickly fills with patrons, mostly members of Atlanta's downtown business community and tourists. The late "Deacon" Lyndell Burton founded this landmark restaurant in 1930, during the Great Depression. Burton moved to Atlanta when he was a young teenager and immediately set out in pursuit of his dream of owning a restaurant. He worked in several Atlanta restaurants and, by age 21, was a highly regarded chef. Even after he opened his own place, he continued working full-time in more established mainstream restaurants. A very religious and civic-minded man, he also gave freely to both his church and the community. As a result, Burton became affectionately known around town as the "Deacon," and his restaurant became an important anchor in his neighborhood. When Deacon Burton passed away in 1992, ownership of the restaurant transferred to his son, Lenn Storey. A public school teacher, Storey divides his time between running the restaurant and maintaining his day job. His wife Beverly devotes full time to the restaurant, and together they are staying true to the legacy of Deacon Burton. Fried chicken is still the focal point, along with fresh vegetables such as collard greens and lima beans. You can get a full-course meal for less than $5.00. Consistently acknowledged as the city's best soul-food restaurant by numerous publications, Deacon Burton's Soul Food should definitely be on your calendar for any visit to Atlanta.

PASCHAL'S HOTEL & RESTAURANT

Location: 830 Martin Luther King, Jr., Blvd.

Telephone: (404) 577-3150

Proprietor: James and Ronald Paschal

Dress: Classy

Menu: Southern/Continental

Price: Modest

Hours: Daily: 11:00 A.M-11:00 P.M.

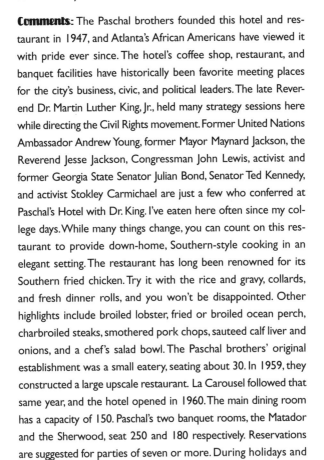

Comments: The Paschal brothers founded this hotel and restaurant in 1947, and Atlanta's African Americans have viewed it with pride ever since. The hotel's coffee shop, restaurant, and banquet facilities have historically been favorite meeting places for the city's business, civic, and political leaders. The late Reverend Dr. Martin Luther King, Jr., held many strategy sessions here while directing the Civil Rights movement. Former United Nations Ambassador Andrew Young, former Mayor Maynard Jackson, the Reverend Jesse Jackson, Congressman John Lewis, activist and former Georgia State Senator Julian Bond, Senator Ted Kennedy, and activist Stokley Carmichael are just a few who conferred at Paschal's Hotel with Dr. King. I've eaten here often since my college days. While many things change, you can count on this restaurant to provide down-home, Southern-style cooking in an elegant setting. The restaurant has long been renowned for its Southern fried chicken. Try it with the rice and gravy, collards, and fresh dinner rolls, and you won't be disappointed. Other highlights include broiled lobster, fried or broiled ocean perch, charbroiled steaks, smothered pork chops, sauteed calf liver and onions, and a chef's salad bowl. The Paschal brothers' original establishment was a small eatery, seating about 30. In 1959, they constructed a large upscale restaurant. La Carousel followed that same year, and the hotel opened in 1960. The main dining room has a capacity of 150. Paschal's two banquet rooms, the Matador and the Sherwood, seat 250 and 180 respectively. Reservations are suggested for parties of seven or more. During holidays and major events such as homecomings and graduations in the Atlanta University complex, get there early! One of the few African American-owned hotels in the country, Paschal's is a must visit during your Atlanta stay.

SATTERWHITE'S RESTAURANT & CATERING

Location: 851 Oak St. NW / 3131 Campbellton Rd.
Telephone: (404) 756-0963 / 344-6401
Proprietor: Bennie Satterwhite
Dress: Casual
Menu: Southern
Price: Very Modest
Hours: Mon.–Sat.: 11:30 A.M.–8:30 P.M.;
Sun.: 12:00 P.M.–6:00 P.M.

Comments: Bennie Satterwhite served in the Marine Corps during the early 1950s where, after graduating from the Corps' Food Services School, he cooked in an officers' mess. Later, he went on to Atlanta's Marriott Hotel, learned the business end of the restaurant industry, and eventually became head chef. Realizing a lifelong dream, he opened his first restaurant, Satterwhite's, in 1990. The enterprise floundered somewhat in its first few months until Satterwhite won a catering contract from Morehouse College during freshman orientation week. This first contract helped launch the restaurant, which has since become an important part of its southwest Atlanta community. The business is very much a family affair. Satterwhite's wife Almedia works the register, and his son Michael is the head chef. Another son, Fernando, manages their restaurant on Campbellton Road. Both locations are great choices. The first is convenient to the Atlanta University complex, the second about 20 minutes from downtown. Each has a menu that includes entrees such as liver and onions, oxtail, barbecue chicken, and fried catfish, whiting, and flounder. Satterwhite's also does a thriving catering business with clients from Atlanta's professional community and the faculty and staff of the Clark Atlanta University Center. You'll find the hospitality at Satterwhite's outstanding and the food superb.

24

THELMA'S KITCHEN

Location: 190 Luckie St.
Telephone: (404) 688-5855
Proprietor: Thelma Grundy
Dress: Casual/Classy
Menu: Southern
Price: Very Modest
Hours: Mon.–Fri.: 7:30 A.M.–4:30 P.M.

Comments: Ambience and chic dining are not the order of the day here—just down-home cooking at its finest! A small serving line up front has a display case where you'll find piping hot entrees such as country-fried steak, barbecue chicken, roast beef, baked ham, and okra cakes. The room seats about 70. It's a good thing, too, because around noon the restaurant is teeming with patrons from the downtown business district. Thelma Grundy started out with a hot-dog stand in the early 1960s, and she has owned restaurants in different locations throughout the city ever since. In recent years, she has established quite a following in her Luckie Street location. Each member of her family has lent a hand. Thelma's husband Riley recently came in to help oversee the business after retiring from 35 years of service with a local printing company. David and Joseph Grundy alternate with their mother as chefs in the kitchen. Thelma's is not only a staple for Atlanta's business community, but also a favorite among local sports figures as well. Atlanta Braves star David Justice is one of her most loyal customers. Heavyweight boxing champion Evander Holyfield is a regular. When Atlanta Hawks journeyman player Enis Whatley stopped by to chat during my interview with Mrs. Grundy, he indicated that he eats all of his pregame meals here. As of this writing, there has been much debate within the local media concerning yet another relocation, this time related to construction for the 1996 Summer Olympics. I hope this doesn't occur, but if it does, Mrs. Grundy's patrons will certainly follow. Grits and eggs with either salmon cakes or sausage are the most-requested breakfast entrees. The fried chicken is crisp on the outside, moist and tender inside. During the lunch hour between 11:30 A.M. and 1:00 P.M., getting a seat may be difficult; however, I've found the period between 1:00 P.M. and 2:30 P.M. to be an excellent time to grab a bite here.

DANCING

CHIT CHAT RESTAURANT AND LOUNGE

Location: 2920 Ember Dr. (Decatur, Ga.)
Telephone: (404) 243-8182
Clientele: Mature Adult
Format: R & B
Calendar: Live Entertainment
Thurs.–Sat.; Dancing Wed.–Sun.
Cover/Minimum: Yes/No
Dress: Casual/Classy

Comments: The Chit Chat Restaurant and Lounge is one of Dekalb County's most popular dance spots. As the name implies, it has always been a favorite place for networking, from the moment the Gribble family opened the club in 1985. Its two dance floors are filled to capacity on any given weekend. Professionals and blue-collar workers alike, they all come here to unwind. Local R & B vocalist Barbara Hall is a mainstay at the club. T. C. Jason, former member of the SOS Band, and his group, Smooth Waye, are also regularly featured. Located just ten minutes from downtown Atlanta, this is an excellent choice for a change of pace and an opportunity to meet residents of outlying Dekalb County.

26

RUPERT'S

Location: 3330 Piedmont Rd. NE
Telephone: (404) 266-9834
Clientele: Young/Mature Adult
Format: Top 40
Calendar: Live Entertainment Tues.–Sat.
Cover/Minimum: Yes/No
Dress: Classy

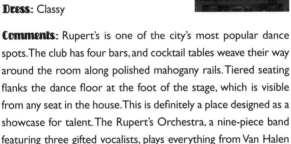

Comments: Rupert's is one of the city's most popular dance spots. The club has four bars, and cocktail tables weave their way around the room along polished mahogany rails. Tiered seating flanks the dance floor at the foot of the stage, which is visible from any seat in the house. This is definitely a place designed as a showcase for talent. The Rupert's Orchestra, a nine-piece band featuring three gifted vocalists, plays everything from Van Halen to Whitney. Rupert's is a fun place full of appreciative fans and one of the few venues in the Southeast where you can dance to top 40 hits played by a live band on almost a nightly basis.

27

THE VIXEN CABARET

Location: 195 Luckie St. NE
Telephone: (404) 523-5895
Clientele: Young/Mature Adult
Format: R & B/House/Jazz/Comedy
Calendar: Live Jazz & Comedy
Fri.–Sat.; Dancing Wed.–Sat.
Cover/Minimum: Yes/No
Dress: Classy

Comments: The Vixen Cabaret was founded in November 1992 to provide Atlanta with a versatile entertainment center featuring R & B, jazz, and comedy. The building in which it is located was constructed by RKO Pictures Corporation for screening motion pictures, the most notable being *Gone with the Wind*. In the 1930s, this area on Luckie Street was known as "Film Row." In recent years, the building has housed several different nightclubs. With more than 12,000 square feet of space, The Vixen Cabaret easily accommodates a ravenous public. The first floor includes a small room where upwards of 50 lucky patrons can experience some of the city's top comedy routines. Another room adjacent to the comedy theater features live jazz. Yet another serves as a sports bar, a popular choice for patrons who favor chats between sports events. Walk upstairs, and you enter the frenetic domain of hip hop, house, and R & B music. Many enjoy this exciting array of choices and spend the evening dancing upstairs for a while, catching a gut-busting comedy routine, then sitting back for some soothing jazz. According to co-owner Gregory Bouquett and manager J. J. Brown, the Vixen recently produced a television pilot, and they hope to broadcast a live dance and talent show from the club each Wednesday night. Many visiting celebrities have dropped in to find out why Atlanta natives are raving about this place. Look along the walls, and you'll see a number of them: comedian Martin Lawrence, NBA star "Shaq" O'Neal, Atlanta Braves slugger David Justice, and former heavyweight champion Evander Holyfield, to name a few. This is definitely one of the best entertainment choices in the city!

V'S ON PEACHTREE

Location: 320 Peachtree St. NE
Telephone: (404) 522-3021
Clientele: Mature Adult
Format: R & B
Calendar: Dancing Tues.–Sat.
Cover/Minimum: Yes (Fri.–Sat.)/No
Dress: Classy

Comments: James Virgil has been a fixture among Atlanta club owners for almost two decades. He got his start throwing house parties in the basement of his Chicago home during the early 1970s. He noticed that he had such a flair for putting on parties that people were willing to pay to attend, and, on the advice of friends, opened his first club, the Appollo. He fell in love with a club he visited in Atlanta while on vacation and negotiated its purchase the very next day. He found some partners who shared his vision and relocated to Atlanta shortly after the deal was set. He renamed the club Mr. V's Figure 8 and experienced immediate success. The club enjoyed enormous popularity from 1978 to 1987. In 1985, Virgil and some partners whom he later bought out opened V's on Peachtree. The club has been an important R & B dance venue in downtown Atlanta ever since. A conversation with "Mr. V" reveals a man who has transformed his passion for the club and restaurant business to an equally strong passion for passing on his expertise to a new generation of entrepreneurs. To this end, he established PYC (Package Your Concept) Enterprises in 1990 and has written a book, *Secret to a Million Dollar Night Club/Restaurant*. He is currently working on an autobiography in hopes that others may want to follow in his path. His legacy is already well recognized by many young Atlanta entrepreneurs. Gregory Bouquett, co-owner of the popular Vixen Cabaret, credits Virgil as having paved the way for African American club owners in Atlanta. V's on Peachtree is still one of his defining achievements. This intimate dance spot has the ambience of a smartly decorated living room. Many Atlantans hold V's among their favorite dance clubs, a place where weekends resemble house parties of old.

BIRMINGHAM, ALABAMA

When many Americans think of Birmingham, what comes to mind are the vivid scenes from the 1960s when the city was a major battleground in the struggle for civil rights. The Birmingham Civil Rights Institute, founded in 1992, recaptures some of those historic moments. Standing in front of the building is a statue of the Reverend Fred L. Shuttlesworth, who worked closely with the Reverend Dr. Martin Luther King, Jr., to steer a course of nonviolent resistance. Inside, a map displays the route that Freedom Riders took in blazing a trail of desegregation throughout the South. In another display, Rosa Parks takes a historic front seat in Montgomery. Yet another shows the bombing of the 16th Street Baptist Church, an infamous event that claimed the lives of four children. The latter display is adjacent to a window overlooking this majestic and historic church.

At the nearby Alabama Jazz Hall of Fame, you'll learn about John T. "Fess" Whatley, the leader of the city's first jazz band and a legendary teacher at the city's first African American high school, the Industrial School. His students during the 1930s and 1940s went on to work with such great bandleaders as Count Basie, Cab Calloway, Duke Ellington, and Billie Holiday. Some of Birmingham's most-celebrated jazz musicians also include Erskine Hawkins, trumpeter and big bandleader, the talented Clarke family (Babe, Chuck, Peter, and Richard), the late jazz drummer extraordinaire Jo Jones, and the late jazz innovator, Sun Ra. Birmingham native Clarence "Pinetop" Smith was one of the outstanding blues pianists of the 1930s.

Mayor Richard Arrington, Jr., has been at the helm of the city since 1979. His administration has facilitated the development of both the Civil Rights Institute and the Jazz Hall of Fame as well as a far-reaching program of urban renewal. A key installment in this effort was the city's revitalization of the 4th Avenue Business District, the center of African American commerce during the early part of the century. Birmingham is a city chock full of history, with a progressive view towards the future.

MUSIC

22ND STREET JAZZ CAFE

Location: 22nd Ave. N and 7th St. S
Telephone: (205) 252-0407
Clientele: Young/Mature Adult
Format: Jazz/Blues/Folk
Calendar: Live Entertainment
Wed., Fri.–Sat.
Cover/Minimum: Yes/Yes (1 drink)
Dress: Casual/Classy

Comments: A small, loft-style club, 22nd Street Jazz Cafe is located on Birmingham's Southside. It's a two-story venue with white-and-purple walls and small, sturdy tables throughout. A stained-glass window graces the front of the club. Several wooden beams span across an opening in the ceiling that provides a glimpse of the second-floor lounge area. Pink fluorescent lights trace heart shapes around mirrors behind the bar. A mural on one wall, next to the bandstand, shows a tuxedo-clad quartet with trumpet, sax, upright bass, and drums poised to play. The band performs in a slightly recessed cubicle in the front of the room. Only the drummer is partially obscured from view from one corner of the room. The second floor is a hideaway for those who prefer intimate conversation. A rail forms a protective barrier around the cutout in the center of the floor. One-third of the room is devoted to a dance floor, which leaves just enough space for eight or nine tables. Only a limited view of the stage is available from this location. Ona Watson and the Champagne Band are frequent headliners. During my visit, Watson, fresh off a tour with Grover Washington, displayed a smooth balladeer style in front of a versatile quartet featuring Don Curry on bass, Daryl Curry on drums, Steve Torock on sax, and C. C. Brown on keyboards. They captured the house with a repertoire ranging from old R & B standards to contemporary to classical jazz. The Tony Lombardo Quartet with Cindy Jones and the Bo Berry Quartet also are popular draws. Birmingham has come to rely on 22nd Street Jazz Cafe as its most consistent jazz and blues venue.

DINING

DREAMLAND BAR-B-QUE

Location: 1427 14th Ave. S
Telephone: (205) 933-2133
Proprietor: Jeanette Bishop-Hall and Bobby Underwood
Dress: Casual/Classy
Menu: Barbecue
Price: Modest
Hours: Mon.–Thurs.: 10:00 A.M.–10:00 P.M.;
Fri.–Sat.: 10:00 A.M.–12:00 A.M.; Sun.: 12:00 P.M.–9:00 P.M.

Comments: When Mayor Arrington's staffers at the Southside Neighborhood Association approached Jeannette Hall about opening a second Dreamland Bar-B-Que in Birmingham, she was very apprehensive. They wanted a big-name restaurant as a marquis addition to the Southside neighborhood, something to add momentum to their efforts to reclaim the area. Hall already had thought about expanding on the success of her original restaurant in Tuscaloosa, even to the point of researching areas in Atlanta as possible locations. Birmingham was not what she had in mind, but after a great deal of soul searching and prayer, Hall consented. Bobby Underwood, a retired dentist passionate about barbecue, had been a Dreamland customer for years and had always secretly nurtured a dream to own a restaurant. Together, they introduced the second Dreamland to Birmingham. It paid immediate dividends to the Southside neighborhood. With concurrent renovations to the park and surrounding buildings by the Southside Neighborhood Association, the area experienced a complete turnaround, so much so that it has been the subject of media exposure throughout the United States. In addition to being an invaluable social investment, the restaurant has paid economic dividends as well. Great barbecue and great teamwork between private citizens and local government can do wondrous things. Make this one a special stop when visiting the city. (For more description of food, see also Dreamland, Tuscaloosa.)

DANCING

FRENCH QUARTERS

Location: 1630 2nd Ave. N
Telephone: (205) 322-1700
Clientele: Young/Mature Adult
Format: R & B/Jazz/Blues
Calendar: Live Entertainment Wed., Fri.–Sun.
Cover/Minimum: Yes/No
Dress: Classy

Comments: The French Quarters is Birmingham's premier show-case lounge and dance club. The club has a format like many in the Southeast, offering multiple venues to accommodate the larg-est-possible customer base. But the French Quarters also offers a bit of a twist on the usual theme: two floors with distinctly different entertainment options. The first floor is the larger of the venues, accommodating more than 400 patrons. The room is dominated by a big dance floor. On one side, amphitheater-style seating cascades down towards the dance floor. Another section of the room provides maroon-velvet lounge chairs ar-rayed about small cocktail tables. This is the area of choice for the younger patrons of the French Quarters. The room kicks to hip hop, house, and contemporary R & B with a steady progres-sion of party-goers throughout the night. The room upstairs is what really sets the French Quarters apart, though. M. E., a five-piece band with four alternating vocalists, is part of a musical stable that makes this club a throwback to the 1960s, before disco became king. A tight quintet, M. E. literally has patrons standing in line to get a seat on the second floor. Vocalist Ed-ward Whatley croons and moans in a voice so commanding that at first one wonders if Luther Vandross somehow slipped in un-noticed. Cassandra Wilkerson sings one line, "Love should'a brought you home last night," and men throw money at her feet. The French Connection band is the other half of the club's week-end attraction. Both bands alternate between touring the region and playing the French Quarters. Pizazz is featured each Wednes-day, playing a hot brand of contemporary jazz. Wynton Marsalis has sat in twice during the past year. This is the stop for many sports celebrities who are visiting the city as well as for mem-bers of the local Birmingham Barons baseball team.

MUSIC

THE CHUKKER

Location: 2161 6th St.
Telephone: (205) 391-0708
Clientele: Young/Mature Adult
Format: Jazz/Blues/Alternative/Folk/World Beat
Calendar: Live Entertainment Thurs.–Sat.
Cover/Minimum: Yes/No
Dress: Casual/Classy

Comments: The Chukker has been everything from a biker bar to a restaurant. In its current iteration, it happens to be Tuscaloosa's only consistent jazz and blues club. It's also one of the most unusual clubs I've seen. The Chukker is divided into two narrow rooms. Pool tables and pin-ball machines recall the club's early years as a haven for bikers. The walls are covered with long psychedelic murals, and the ceiling in one room is covered with a painting called the "Sistene Chukker," done by a local artist during the heyday of the hippie movement. Cocktail tables, in keeping with the theme throughout, are covered with abstract art. The atmosphere of the club varies with the musical format. On Mondays, the club features Percussion Night where patrons are encouraged to bring their own. According to owner Ludvic Goubet, dreadlocks and bare feet are the order of the day. Tuesday nights bring out the avant garde for poetry readings, while the first Friday after Christmas is traditionally reserved for the Chukker Nation Reunion, a group of Vietnam vets and bikers who come in from all areas of the country to commemorate the time in the 1970s when they met at the Chukker each Friday night. As eclectic as the club seems, the Chukker also has a chameleonlike ability to transform itself into a top jazz and blues draw. The late Sun Ra played three concerts here in April 1992. McCoy Tyner's December 1992 concert at the Chukker was his first in Alabama. The legendary John Ned "Johnny" Shines played here regularly before he passed away in 1993. More recently, the club featured the West Coast style of bluesman Philip Walker. Just how important is this club to the Tuscaloosa/Birmingham area? The Alabama Blues Society puts it this way in their June 1994 newsletter: "Thanks again to Ludovic Goubet and the Chukker for continuing to bring top-quality music to our state."

DINING

DREAMLAND BAR-B-QUE

Location: 5535 15th Ave. E
Telephone: (205) 758-8135
Proprietor: The Bishop Family
Dress: Casual
Menu: Barbecue
Price: Modest
Hours: Mon.–Thurs.:
10:00 A.M.–9:00 P.M.; Fri.–Sat.: 10:00 A.M.–10:00 P.M.

Comments: John and Lillie Bishop founded Dreamland Bar-B-Que in 1958. Except for a few coats of fresh paint, the outside of the building has changed little since then. The sturdy red-brick-and-pine structure is surrounded by wooden picket fences on a half-acre lot. Inside, the restaurant walls are alive with posters, photographs, and license plates. Some photos show the Bishop clan, while others profile visiting celebrities such as Miami Dolphins football coach Don Shula, country singer Reba McEntire, and Florida State football coach Bobby Bowden. Hundreds of bags of potato chips and Dreamland Bar-B-Que sauce (sold by the quart) line the shelf behind a long serving counter. An old wood-burning stove and piles of hickory, oak, and pecan wood stacked in front of the barbecue pit all add to the rustic ambience. The dining room is expansive, but only seats about 60. Until 1980, this was just a popular neighborhood haunt. They served a full menu, sometimes including chitterlings. But the demand for pork barbecue grew so much that the restaurant had to start serving it exclusively to keep pace with the orders. When Lillie became ill, her daughter, Jeanette Bishop-Hall, was called in to run the business, and the restaurant has continued to soar. It has been featured on CNN, ESPN, "NBC News with Tom Brokaw" and "The Oprah Winfrey Show," to name just a few! *Atlanta* magazine, *Elle* magazine, and the *New York Times* have each done articles on it. The restaurant uses a cut of rib "three and one-half down." The meat is barbecued precisely 45 minutes, marinated in its own juices and Dreamland's special sauce. This is one of the Southeast's true treasures. If you're traveling on I-20 East/59 South, take exit 73 (McFarland Boulevard) and turn left onto McFarland. Go to the fourth signal and turn left onto Jug Factory Road. Follow the sign at the top of the hill.

HOUSTON, TEXAS

Houston's diversity is illustrated by its large African American, Asian, and Hispanic populations, and the city proudly reflects the influences of each. Its annual celebration of Juneteenth commemorates one of the most important dates and events in Texas history, June 19, 1865, when slaves in the state were emancipated. One year later, nine former slaves founded the Antioch Missionary Baptist Church, the city's first African American church.

Texas Southern University is Houston's only "historically black college." Relatively new compared to most, it was founded in 1949. Barbara Jordan, one of the university's most distinguished graduates, has served as an inspiration to young African American politicians and to women of all races nationwide. She is associated with several milestones: first African American elected to the Texas State Senate since Reconstruction and first African American woman elected to Congress. Her accomplishments as a congresswoman from Houston's 18th Congressional District set a standard that was followed by her successor, the late Mickey Leland, then by former Congressman Craig Washington, and now, by Congresswoman Sheila Jackson Lee.

Former Houston Oiler quarterback Warren Moon is perhaps the city's most celebrated athlete, not only for his accomplishments on the football field, but also for his involvement in the community and for his prolific works of charity. His social activism serves as a model for those unwilling simply to sit on the sidelines.

Longtime residents of Houston fondly recall a period when the city's numerous wards were home to elegant nightclubs and theaters. Blues legends such as Sam "Lightnin'" Hopkins and Willie Mae "Big Mama" Thornton, along with jazz big-bandleader Illinois Jacquet, dominated the music scene. During the late 1950s, African American entrepreneur Don Robey owned both the highly regarded Bronze Peacock Club and one of the first African American record labels, Duke/Peacock, which recorded artists such as Johnny Ace, Junior Parker, and B. B. King.

Houston remains a place that intrigues and excites. Although navigating by way of the Interstate 610 Loop can seem formidable at first, if you relax, you'll discover that the Loop provides infinite ways to experience the cultural offerings of this

MUSIC

BILLY BLUES

Location: 6025 Richmond Ave.
Telephone: (713) 266-9294
Clientele: Young/Mature Adult
Format: Blues
Calendar: Live Entertainment Nightly
Cover/Minimum: Yes/No
Dress: Casual/Classy

Comments: You'll count a visit to Billy Blues among your most memorable experiences. The first indication is the huge blue saxophone nestled against the front of the building. Next comes the valet-parking attendant, an unusual sight for a self-respecting blues joint. The reception area is staffed with hostesses selling club memorabilia and Billy Blues barbecue sauce. You'll also find the more traditional staple of photographs depicting blues legends such as Clarence "Gatemouth" Brown, Guitar Slim, and Sam "Lightnin'" Hopkins. The main dining room and bar are alive with red bricks and still more photos and blackboards listing their "Blues Plate Specials" and the month's entertainment schedule. For contrast, go into the blues room at the back. Here is the ambience of a classic blues club. The whole room, with its hardwood floor and thick wooden beams, is designed around the stage, and virtually every seat is a good one. On my initial visit, I caught a show by one of the city's hot young blues bands, Mark May and the Agitators. This is a place to settle into a comfortable seat, sample a great brisket sandwich, and hunker down, Texas blues style. Billy Blues has become Houston's premier blues club by virtue of its classy supper-club format and its staggering array of blues talent. According to a club spokesman, Billy Blues' mission is to provide pecan-smoked Texas barbecue and good blues. They also support "Blues Stage" on National Public Radio. Founded in San Antonio in 1990, the Billy Blues Corporation has expanded to locations in Denver, Dallas, and Phoenix. Another venture with the legendary Antoine's blues club in Austin is scheduled soon. While I'm a definite proponent of retaining our traditional blues clubs as the national treasures they have become, I'm also attracted to the new, sophistocated genre of blues clubs such as Billy Blues. Both types of venue are needed to help keep the blues alive.

C. DAVIS BAR-B-Q

Location: 4833 Reed Rd.
Telephone: (713) 734-9051
Clientele: Mature Adult
Format: Blues
Calendar: Live Entertainment Tues. & Sun.
Cover/Minimum: Yes/No
Dress: Casual/Classy

Comments: This "hole in the wall" has been the scene of one of the city's most consistent blues jams for more than two decades. Tucked away in Houston's Third Ward, C. Davis Bar-B-Q is a throwback to the great blues places of the 1930s and 1940s. Clarence Davis, who had been a truck driver in the Houston area for a number of years, couldn't find the kind of barbecue he liked in area restaurants, so he decided to open his own place in 1971. The taste of Davis's barbecue is achieved by slow-cooking the meat (14 hours for brisket) over oak and pecan wood, then adding his secret tomato-based sauce. Shortly after it opened, Davis decided that his barbecue place should also offer the blues because, as he says, "blues and barbecue go together." He started out with zydeco, then switched to blues, Texas style. Joe Nettles, a top-flight blues organist on the Houston scene, was one of his first acts. For the last 19 or so years, veteran blues guitarist I. J. Gosey has been the featured act. When asked what has kept him here all this time, Gosey replies, "You see the same faces for almost 20 years, lose a few, gain a few." He also likes the atmosphere and the fact that the crowd allows him the freedom to play what he wants, "whether it's jazz, blues, country, or whatever." Gosey has been on the Houston music scene since the mid-1950s. As a studio musician for the old Duke/Peacock label, he backed up legends such as Buddy Ace, Clarence "Gatemouth" Brown, Junior Parker, "Big Mama" Thornton, and Joe Tex. Gosey's current band includes Morgan Bouldin on keyboards, Jackie Gordon on drums, and Eugene Hawthorne on bass. Listen to them slide from Texas blues to zydeco to jazz, and you will quickly understand why the *Houston Press* says that "the blues is alive and well out in Sunnyside." *Texas* magazine ranks C. Davis Bar-B-Q among "the hand full of blues bars that offer blues the way it used to be."

CÉZANNE

Location: 4100 Montrose Blvd.
Telephone: (713) 867-7992
Clientele: Young/Mature Adult
Format: Jazz
Calendar: Live Entertainment Thurs.–Sat.
Cover/Minimum: Yes/Yes (1 drink per set)
Dress: Casual/Classy

Comments: Cézanne is one of the few clubs in Houston with a format dedicated exclusively to jazz. According to club booking agent Dave Catney, the first time he saw the tiny room on the second floor above the Black Labrador Restaurant, he fell in love with it and talked the management into letting him book jazz acts. A jazz pianist who recently recorded "Reality Road" on the Justice Records label, Catney frequently performs at the club. He also books acts he knows are just on the verge of mainstream popularity. Many are schoolmates from his North Texas State University days. Some of the most recent acts at Cézanne include pianist/composer Bill Cunliffe, a longtime member of the Buddy Rich Orchestra, saxophonist Bob Belden, a Blue Note recording artist, and Steve Huffsteter, a veteran trumpet/fluglehorn player who has worked on more than 60 albums. The music at Cézanne ranges from straightahead to classical jazz. While the words "intimate" and "cozy" are often overused in describing a jazz club, they are tailor-made for Cézanne. With its wood paneling and living-room ambience, it's the perfect venue for experiencing jazz.

39

CODY'S ROOFTOP JAZZ BAR & GRILL

Location: 3400 Montrose Blvd.
Telephone: (713) 522-9747
Clientele: Young/Mature Adult
Format: Jazz/R & B
Calendar: Live Entertainment Nightly
Cover/Minimum: Yes/Yes (Fri.–Sat./1 purchase per set)
Dress: Classy

Comments: Opened in 1976, Cody's has long been among Houston's most popular dance and supper clubs. The decor is upscale, and the panoramic view of the city is fantastic. Some patrons opt for a table in the main dining room with a bird's-eye view of the band, while others choose the glass-encased or open-air patio. I spent a Saturday evening here and enjoyed a performance by the Mysti Day band. Mysti Day, who formerly recorded on the Virgin label, leads a group of talented musicians whose repertoire ranges from Motown music to jazz and blues. Day has a voice that excels on old standards from the Jackson 5's early years and is equally adept at today's top 40 hits. Background vocalist Anne Mundy, keyboard player Ronald Cole, sax man Gerald Spikes, and drummer Ernest Walker round out the band. Get here before 9:00 P.M., and you're almost assured of choice seating. Most seats in the dining room offer a good view of the band, but if you come much later, you'll find that the club quickly fills, on many nights approaching its capacity of 400 plus. Whether you're in the mood for fine continental dining, dancing, or taking in a rooftop view, this is a supper club you'll count among your favorites.

ETTA'S LOUNGE & RESTAURANT

Location: 5120 Scott St.

Telephone: (713) 528-2611

Clientele: Young/Mature Adult

Format: Blues

Calendar: Live Entertainment Sun.

Cover/Minimum: Yes/No

Dress: Casual/Classy

Comments: Whenever I venture into one of these old-style blues clubs, I wonder how long places like Etta's will continue to dot the nation's landscape. Forever, I hope. But when you talk to the staff at Etta's, they lament that they're not as active as they once were, having scaled down from offering live entertainment all weekend to just on Sunday evenings. The economy is the culprit, they are quick to point out. Nevertheless, Etta's continues to be an important club in Houston that one evening each week. On Sundays, the venerable sax man Grady Gaines descends on Etta's with his Upsetters Band and transforms the place. The club is bare on the outside, not even yielding its name to the casual observer. Inside, it's also bare, but spacious and attractive in a simple way. Against this backdrop, Gaines and the Upsetters hold court for an appreciative audience comprised of Houstonians from throughout the city. Playing a range of music from Texas blues to R & B, the band sizzles on tunes by artists such as Muddy Waters, Joe Tex, Al Green, and Marvin Gaye.

41

EVENING SHADOWS CLUB

Location: 3936 Old Spanish Trail
Telephone: (713) 748-7683
Clientele: Young/Mature Adult
Format: Blues/Jazz/R & B
Calendar: Live Entertainment Tues., Thurs.–Sun.
Cover/Minimum: Yes/Yes (2 drinks)
Dress: Casual/Classy

Comments: Mrs. V. Johnson has been a fixture on the Houston business scene for more than 20 years. Most widely known for her barber and beauty colleges throughout the city, she founded the Evening Shadows Club in 1990. It's a classy little blues and jazz lounge with subdued shades of blue and green throughout. The main room is snug up against the stage, while a small alcove is nestled adjacent to it. Both allow excellent views of the band, and the club overall has superb acoustics. Patrons of this hideaway really enjoy their music, enthusiastically responding to hot riffs, a vocalist's nuance, or a rousing bass solo. I caught an outstanding set performed by one of Houston's popular straightahead groups, Spontaneous Jazz. With James McNeil on vocals and congas, the group really excels on old standards such as "Autumn Leaves" and "My Funny Valentine." Russel Sledge on upright, Francis Reed on tenor sax and keyboards, Terry Thomas also on keyboards, and Malcolm Pinson on drums round out the band. They combine in a straightahead groove that will leave you riveted to your seat. The Ray Brown Band also is a local favorite delivering jazz and R & B hits each weekend. While these two bands give you ample reason to come down to Evening Shadows, three of the top blues artists in the city highlight the entertainment offered here. The reigning queen of Houston blues, Trudy Lynn, headlines every Friday and Sunday, while Houston legend Joe "Guitar" Hughes holds court each Tuesday, and the venerable Grady Gaines reigns supreme on Thursdays. According to club manager Curtis Dixon, the club has been a hit from the very beginning. Its personality changes each night because each of the headliners has his or her own following. Whether your choice is blues, jazz, or R & B, Evening Shadows is a great place to hear some of the best music in the city. Put this club on your "A list."

REDDI ROOM

Location: 2662 White Oak Dr.
Telephone: (713) 868-6188
Clientele: Young/Mature Adult
Format: Blues/R & B
Calendar: Live Entertainment Wed.–Sat.
Cover/Minimum: Yes/No
Dress: Casual/Classy

Comments: The late Bill Stebbins flew combat missions in the South Pacific in World War II, and, like many young Americans of that period, his experiences during the war years expanded his horizons profoundly. One of the experiences that touched him most deeply was the discovery of the blues, something he picked up from fellow squadron members. After the war, he owned and operated several lounges, but in 1985, he found his true calling when he established this classic blues club. According to Stebbins's widow, Edna Besiant, the Reddi Room adheres to a format featuring Delta blues because, for her, "the music of the Delta gets right down to the origin, the history of the blues." Milton Hopkins, former lead guitarist for B. B. King, has been playing the Reddi Room for the past eight years. In fact, he has "grown the audience" himself, expanding the audience and their knowledge of the blues. Hopkins and his band are equally at home playing blues and R & B. The band features Ardis Turner on vocals and drums, Robert Phelps on sax, Jimmy Hunter on bass, and Malcom Penson on drums. Joe James, an R & B artist well known for his propensity for doing head stands on the table tops while performing, also is regularly featured at the club. Although the focus at the Reddi Room is on local blues acts, national recording artists such as B. B. King often drop by when doing concerts in the city. A TWA customer service representative by day and a blues lounge owner by night, Besiant has her hands full keeping the Reddi Room at the forefront of blues in Houston. Judging by the periodic features on Houston local television stations and within the Houston press, I'd say that this Grambling State University graduate is more than up to the task. Stop by on any weekend, and you'll find a room full of appreciative patrons who heartily agree. Many of them refer to the Reddi Room as the best little blues joint in Houston!

43

DINING

DREXLER'S BARBECUE

Location: 2020 Dowling St.
Telephone: (713) 752-0008
Proprietor: The Drexler Family
Dress: Casual/Classy
Menu: Barbecue
Price: Modest
Hours: Tues.–Thurs.:
10:00 A.M.–6:00 P.M.; Fri.–Sat.: 10:00 A.M.–8:00 P.M.

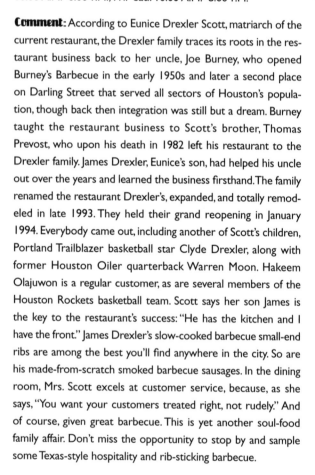

Comment: According to Eunice Drexler Scott, matriarch of the current restaurant, the Drexler family traces its roots in the restaurant business back to her uncle, Joe Burney, who opened Burney's Barbecue in the early 1950s and later a second place on Darling Street that served all sectors of Houston's population, though back then integration was still but a dream. Burney taught the restaurant business to Scott's brother, Thomas Prevost, who upon his death in 1982 left his restaurant to the Drexler family. James Drexler, Eunice's son, had helped his uncle out over the years and learned the business firsthand. The family renamed the restaurant Drexler's, expanded, and totally remodeled in late 1993. They held their grand reopening in January 1994. Everybody came out, including another of Scott's children, Portland Trailblazer basketball star Clyde Drexler, along with former Houston Oiler quarterback Warren Moon. Hakeem Olajuwon is a regular customer, as are several members of the Houston Rockets basketball team. Scott says her son James is the key to the restaurant's success: "He has the kitchen and I have the front." James Drexler's slow-cooked barbecue small-end ribs are among the best you'll find anywhere in the city. So are his made-from-scratch smoked barbecue sausages. In the dining room, Mrs. Scott excels at customer service, because, as she says, "You want your customers treated right, not rudely." And of course, given great barbecue. This is yet another soul-food family affair. Don't miss the opportunity to stop by and sample some Texas-style hospitality and rib-sticking barbecue.

FAMILY CAFE

Location: 2712 Blodgett St.
Telephone: (713) 520-8444
Proprietor: Mary Gillum
Dress: Casual/Classy
Menu: Soul Food
Price: Very Modest
Hours: Mon.–Fri.: 6:00 A.M.–6:00 P.M.;
Sat.–Sun.: 6:00 P.M.–5:00 P.M.

Comments: The late Henry Gillum was a truck driver for the Grocery Supply Company for 30 years. Uncertain about what to do on retiring in 1978, he talked the management into letting him run the company's employee cafeteria. He then coaxed his wife Annie Mae, a longtime private cook, into coming to work with him. Next, he lured his daughter Mary, a Texas Southern University graduate, away from her accounting job by matching her salary and providing the irresistible allure of entrepreneurship. When the Grocery Supply Company decided to eliminate the cafeteria three years later, the Gillums opened their own restaurant on Blodgett Street. After several years of successful operations, Henry Gillum's health began to fail, and he turned the business over to daughter Mary. A third generation of Gillums, Mary's son Amar, manages the restaurant while her other son, Derrick Smith, helps out each summer during his break from mechanical engineering studies at Prairie View A & M University. The loss of Mary's father Henry was difficult to overcome. So was the risk they assumed by undergoing a major renovation that kept them closed for almost six months during 1993 and 1994. They've recently reopened and have rebounded well. This attractive little eatery is located a block from Texas Southern University. Customers come from all areas of Houston society, including members of the Texas State Legislature, faculty and students of Texas Southern and Houston Universities, as well as a host of Houston's professional athletes. The Family Cafe also has been featured in a variety of Houston publications including the *Houston Post* and the African American journal, the *Houston Informer.* Stop by and feast on soulful dishes such as their popular oxtails, ham hocks, collard greens, turnip greens, and peach cobbler. You'll come back for more!

NORRIS RESTAURANT

Location: 2491 S. Braeswood Blvd.
Telephone: (713) 664-9447
Proprietor: Craig and Alveda Allen
Dress: Casual/Classy
Menu: Creole/Cajun/Southern
Price: Modest
Hours: Tues.–Thurs.: 11:00 A.M.–9:00 P.M.;
Fri.–Sat.: 11:00 A.M.–11:00 P.M.; Sun.: 10:00 A.M.–4:00 P.M.

Comments: Craig Allen worked in restaurants since the age of 15 to finance his education and realized during high school that he wanted to own his own place. After earning his college degree from Southern Methodist University, he returned to Houston, worked in real estate for a year, then signed on with the Minfas restaurant chain as a management trainee. In late 1992, Allen left the chain and launched his own restaurant. The Norris Restaurant is attractive and spacious, with a decor accented with brown bricks, pastels, and blue formica tables. The main dining room seats 104, the banquet room 80. There's also a small bar adjacent to the dining room, visible through large picture windows. Every six months or so, the restaurant features paintings of a local artist throughout the dining room and bar, something Allen does to give his place a different look. Owing to its proximity to the Houston Medical Center, the restaurant gets a good crowd for its lunch buffet Mondays through Fridays. The Jazzy Sunday Brunch is also very popular. The menu features a delicious array of cuisine such as "traditional etouffee sauce combined with sauteed shrimp or crawfish & served over rice," jambalaya "(rice, chicken sausage & ham combined with cajun tomatoes to create a Louisiana tradition)," seafood gumbo, and red beans and rice with andouille sausage. Tony Brown, former Congressman Craig Washington, and Congresswoman Sheila Jackson Lee, along with Mayor Bob Lanier, have all come through. The *Houston Post*, the *Chronicle*, and the *Defender* are but a few of the publications that have done features on Norris Restaurant. This is one of the places that you must put on your itinerary when you visit the city.

RJ'S RIB JOINT

Location: 2515 Riverside Dr.
Telephone: (713) 521-9601
Proprietor: Raymond Jordan
Dress: Casual/Classy
Menu: Barbecue/Seafood
Price: Modest
Hours: Mon.–Thurs.:
11:00 A.M.–10:00 P.M.; Fri.–Sat.: 11:00 A.M.–11:00 P.M.

Comments: RJ's Rib Joint is full of surprises, the biggest one being the restaurant's appearance. It occupies the lower level of what could easily pass for a beautiful, private brick residence. The decor is accented by African artwork, hanging plants, ceiling fans, large picture windows with stained-glass inserts, hardwood dining tables, and four small dining areas, one of which is enclosed by glass doors for private parties. It all comes together to create an ambiance that is both airy and cozy. RJ'S varied menu offers yet another surprise. I enjoyed a succulent order of baby back ribs and potato salad; however, RJ's goes a bit beyond the traditional rib-house menu by offering not only barbecue, but also Cajun dishes such as seafood or sausage jambalaya and blackened catfish, and Creole dishes such as shrimp Creole and oyster po-boys. Other seafood dishes include a platter with fried shrimp, oysters, and catfish-stuffed shrimp, and a shrimp-and-crabmeat-stuffed flounder fillet. The restaurant also offers a tantalizing trio of desserts: homemade peach cobbler, cheesecake, and "Bluebell Homemade Ice Cream." Give yourself a special treat and make this restaurant one of your top choices when visiting Houston.

THIS IS IT

Location: 239 W. Gray St.
Telephone: (713) 523-5319
Proprietor: Craig Joseph
Dress: Casual/Classy
Menu: Soul Food
Price: Very Modest
Hours: Mon.–Thurs.:
6:30 A.M.–8:00 P.M.; Fri.–Sat.: 6:30 A.M-10:30 P.M.

Comments: Frank Jones founded This Is It in 1959. Before that, he had a barbecue restaurant in Los Angeles during the 1930s. He and his wife Mattie started out in Houston as a mom-and-pop business, operating for 24 years out of their home at 1003 Andrews Street, in the heart of the Fourth Ward. In response to their enormous popularity, they moved to their current location and built the restaurant from the ground up. Jones retired in 1992, turning This Is It over to his grandson Craig Joseph. Through the years, the restaurant has evolved into Houston's most popular soul-food eatery. It is short on frills but spacious and attractive. A pair of gold records above the doorway commemorates the hits "Mr. Scarface Is Back" and "Till Death Do Us Part." Both were presented to the restaurant by the rap group, the Geto Boys, also products of Houston's Fourth Ward. A celebrity wall depicts past customers such as B. B. King, Johnnie Taylor, and Bobby Womack. According to Joseph, the Reverend Jesse Jackson is also a frequent visitor. In fact, the last time he came, he spent most of the evening waiting on tables and chatting with the guests. This is a place to bring your friends and family, settle into a booth or pull a few tables together, and enjoy a great meal. I made myself right at home and proceeded to dispatch a generous portion of cabbage, pinto beans, and rice and gravy garnished with smothered pork chops. A glass of ice-cold lemonade was just the right complement for the delicious meal. Folks have been repeating this scenario at This Is It for more than three decades. The most popular entrees are the oxtails and chitterlings. Other menu items include meatloaf, pepper steak, turkey wings, lima beans, and candied yams. Put this eatery at the top of your list when visiting the city.

DANCING

CLUB GRAMMY

Location: 2525 Murworth Dr.
Telephone: (713) 668-2239
Clientele: Mature Adult
Format: R & B
Calendar: Live Entertainment Thurs.; Dancing Nightly
Cover/Minimum: Yes/No
Dress: Classy

Comments: Club Grammy occupies a building that has housed a variety of other entertainment establishments. According to Val Takushi, club manager, it was remodeled for Club Grammy to achieve an R & B venue that is upscale and posh. The designers created a two-level, semicircular dance floor surrounded by two rows of cocktail tables. Another level of tables and booths is arrayed in an outer circle around the club. The management also installed the latest lighting effects and a superb sound system. The result is one of Houston's most popular dance settings for a mature crowd whose passion is oldies and contemporary R & B. The club seats about 450. Tuesdays and Fridays are their most popular evenings. Depending on the off-season, you're likely to see any number of Houston Astros, Oilers, or Rockets come through. Every day except Sunday there's a Happy Hour Buffet at 4:00 P.M.; on Sunday, the club offers a Midnight Buffet. Located about two blocks from the Houston Astrodome, Club Grammy is an outstanding choice for an after-game evening out.

49

JACKSON, MISSISSIPPI

The history of Mississippi music is now legend. Arising out of the particularly brutal conditions experienced first by slaves and later by sharecroppers in the state's Delta region, this music came straight from the soul and found expression in African American spirituals, gospel, blues, jazz, and R & B. The region gave birth not only to the music, but also to many of its finest practitioners. Clarksdale produced John Lee Hooker, Junior Parker, and Sam Cooke; Indianola produced Albert King and Riley "B. B." King; and Rolling Fork produced McKinley Morganfield aka Muddy Waters, just to cite a few.

During the early years of the blues, especially between the 1920s and 1950s, one could go to Jackson's Farish Street and hear not only the top blues stars but jazz and emerging R & B artists as well. Jackson has nurtured its share of blues legends. The man many consider to have been the king of Delta blues, Charlie Patton, was born just outside the city in Edwards, Mississippi. Pianist "Little Johnny" Jones, pianist and harmonica player Otis Spann, and guitarist "Boogie" Bill Webb also were Jackson natives.

Today, Jackson's music scene is defined by Malaco Records, an impressive African American label founded in 1965 by Thomas Couch, Stewart Madison, and Wolf Stephenson. Malaco records some of the top gospel and R & B acts in the country. Their roster of gospel stars includes the Georgia Mass Choir, the Gospel Keynotes, the Jackson Southernaires, the Mississippi Mass Choir, the Reverend James Moore, and the Pilgrim Jubilees; their roster of blues and R & B stars includes Bobby "Blue" Bland, Shirley Brown, the late Z. Z. Hill, Denise LaSalle, Latimore, Little Milton, Dorothy Moore, and Johnny Taylor. Jackson State University graduate Cassandra Wilson has emerged as a major force on the jazz scene and is being compared with all jazz legends. Another J.S.U. graduate, guitarist, songwriter, and producer, Vasti Jackson, is one of the country's hot new blues talents.

When you're visiting Jackson, stop by the Smith Robinson Museum and the Mississippi State Museum to catch a glimpse of the city's rich history, and by all means, take advantage of any opportunity to experience Mississippi music, whether it's blues

MUSIC

HAL & MAL'S RESTAURANT & OYSTER BAR

Location: 200 S. Commerce St.
Telephone: (601) 948-0888
Clientele: Young/Mature Adult
Format: Blues/Rock & Roll
Calendar: Live Entertainment Varies
Cover/Minimum: Yes/No
Dress: Casual/Classy

Comments: Hal and Mal's Restaurant & Oyster Bar is located in an old warehouse that once served as one of Jackson's busiest freight depots. In 1986, Malcolm White, his wife Vivian, and his brother Harold leased the entire complex and converted it into Jackson's premier entertainment showcase. Over the years, the club has featured blues stars such as Bobby "Blue" Bland, Otis Clay, the late Albert King, and B. B. King. The Tangents, a blues and R & B group from the Delta, Patrice Moncell, and Miss Molly and the Whips are some of their most popular local acts. The restaurant occupies three rooms in the front of the complex. Each is accented in sea green, and the main dining room displays numerous early transistor radios. Adjacent to the restaurant, but accessible through another entrance, is a small entertainment venue. The carpeted room lined with vinyl booths features a large stage. Beyond this room is yet another entertainment area, simply called the "Big Room." This room spanning almost the entire length of the complex has a hardwood floor and a large concert stage. It holds at least 700, while the smaller room accommodates about 200. A patio in the back, enclosed by a high, red brick wall, provides yet another entertainment option. Besides great music in an intimate setting, an evening at Hal and Mal's also offers a dining experience that stands on its own merits. The best red beans and rice this side of New Orleans, fried or grilled catfish, and seafood platters are but a few of the delights. The desserts include mouth-watering chocolate silk pies and praline ice cream. The restaurant, which seats 90, is open for lunch and dinner Monday through Friday from 11:00 A.M. and for dinner on Saturday from 5:00 P.M. Hal and Mal's has been featured in *Connoisseur*, *Esquire*, the *Mississippi Business Journal*, and the local daily, the *Clarion Ledger*. Stop by, and you'll understand why.

51

NAME OF THE GAME

Location: 2645 Livingstone Rd.
Telephone: (601) 362-8414
Clientele: Young/Mature Adult
Format: Blues/R & B
Calendar: Live Entertainment Wed.–Thurs.; Dancing Fri.–Sat.
Cover/Minimum: No/Yes (1 drink)
Dress: Casual/Classy

Comments: Name of the Game is Jackson's most consistent blues and R & B venue. The club originally opened during the mid-1970s as Caesar's Palace. Jessie Stringer, Sr., and his son Jessie Junior purchased the club in 1985 and renamed it. State-of-the-art sound and lighting systems have been installed as a part of the building's infrastructure. Downstairs, the ambience is accented by cocktail tables draped with red linen, a red-and-black vinyl bar in front of the room, a black ceiling, and red walls. The main bar seats 300. A second bar upstairs accommodating 100 is used for private parties. Local blues recording star Bobby Rush is regularly featured at the club, as is Hazlehurst, Mississippi's R & B recording artist Dorothy Moore. Billy "Soul" Barnes and Willie Clayton head a list of other top blues and R & B acts that have played the room. Regional and national acts include Bobby "Blue" Bland, Tyrone Davis and Denise LaSalle, Latimore, and Marvin Sease. At least once a month, the club holds a special Sunday matinee featuring touring acts. Stringer has been in the club business for more than a decade, and his experience shows in Name of the Game.

52

SOOP'S RESTAURANT & LOUNGE

Location: 3028 W. Northside Dr.

Telephone: (601) 981-1402

Clientele: Mature Adult

Format: Blues/Rock & Roll

Calendar: Live Entertainment Wed.–Thurs.; Dancing Fri.–Sat.

Cover/Minimum: Yes (Thurs.)/No

Dress: Casual/Classy

Comments: Soop's Restaurant & Lounge enjoys broad support from longtime residents of Jackson. Whether they're day laborers, physicians, or schoolteachers, they all come here because of the attractive decor, the relaxed ambience, and the oldies R & B format. Walls painted the deepest shade of black, panel mirrors spanning the entire length of the dance floor, and black-and-white checkerboard tile dominate the room's decor. The lighting bathes the room in a warm glow. Situated along the right wall as you enter are cocktail tables that course along the dance floor and end in a cluster opposite the long bar at the rear. The club seats about 200. Owner Joe Mitchell leads Soop and Company here each Wednesday and Thursday night. The music is white-hot blues and R & B standards from the 1960s, from Z. Z. Hill to Little Milton to Tyrone Davis. The band consists of Mitchell on bass and keyboards, Bernard Johnson, Jr., on lead guitar, Stephen Powell on drums, and Rick Lawson on vocals. Buddy Ace, Joe Blackfoot, Shirley Brown, Willie Clayton, and Dorothy Moore are among the blues and R & B stars who have been featured. Local blues stars Billy "Soul" Barnes, "Cadillac" George Harris, and Tina Diamond have also performed here. Joe Mitchell has long been a fixture on Jackson's music scene; for almost 20 years, he has headed the music department at Callaway High School. His musical career began in the late 1960s as a student at Jackson State University. Nowadays, he's educating other students by day and running one of Jackson's favorite entertainment venues by night.

53

DINING

BULLY'S RESTAURANT

Location: 3118 Livingstone Rd.
Telephone: (601) 362-0484
Proprietor: W. G. Bully
Dress: Casual/Classy
Menu: Soul Food
Price: Very Modest
Hours: Mon.–Thurs.: 11:00 A.M.–6:00 P.M.;
Fri.–Sat.: 11:00 A.M.–8:00 P.M.

Comments: Ask most Jackson residents where you can find the best soul-food fare in the city, and the answer more often than not is Bully's Restaurant—they love the down-home taste of the food and the generous helpings. An entree such as smothered roast beef comes piled high with tender meat and three succulent vegetables. You also get dessert and two cornbread muffins! I tried the roast beef with a side order of mixed greens, butter beans, rice and gravy, and corn bread. By the time I had eaten half of it, I realized that I'd better taste the peach cobbler before I could eat no more. The meal rates among the ten best I've tried since I started work on this book. The restaurant is a small, attractive eatery located less than ten minutes from downtown Jackson. Sit-down diners will find the space a bit cramped; the seating accommodates only about 25. A smaller room at the entrance is where most patrons queue up, because take-out is the order of the day here. Longtime residents of Jackson usually call ahead to order their favorite dishes. It's also best to come early in the day because the most popular dishes sell out quickly. Beef tips and rice, boiled neck bones, and smothered pork chops are the items that normally go fastest. Other entrees include catfish fillets, ham hocks, pan-fried trout, and oxtail. Vegetable selections include fried corn, cabbage, and yams along with homemade desserts such as lemon icebox pie and cheesecake. W. G. Bully founded the restaurant in 1981. His wife Robbie, son Tyrone, and daughter-in-law Grete all lend a hand in the day-to-day operation of the restaurant. Tyrone Bully cites the quality of the food and the dedicated work ethic of each family member as keys to the success of the restaurant. Featured by the *Clarion Ledger* as the city's top soul-food restaurant, Bully's also provides catering services, primarily for family reunions and weddings.

FRANK'S 'World Famous Biscuits' RESTAURANT

Location: 219 N. President St.
Telephone: (601) 354-5357
Proprietor: A. L. Latham
Dress: Casual/Classy
Menu: Southern
Price: Very Modest

Hours: Mon.–Fri.: 6:00 A.M.–4:00 P.M.; Sat.: 6:00 A.M.–2:00 P.M.

Comments: Frank's "World Famous Biscuits" Restaurant is an attractive breakfast and lunch place in downtown Jackson. The interior is decorated in stark white, offset by hardwood tile and oak fixtures throughout. Four dining rooms provide cozy environs for private parties and public fare. Located within walking distance of the Capitol, this is one of the city's most popular dining spots. On my first visit, Mississippi's secretary of state was hosting a private luncheon in an adjacent dining room. Willard Scott, the weatherman on NBC's "Today Show," has featured the restaurant on three different segments over the past four years. It has also been featured in *Entrepreneur Magazine*, the *Jackson Business Journal*, and the *Clarion Ledger*. The restaurant offers breakfast throughout the day. The menu features standard breakfast fare—Southern breakfast fare, that is: grits, eggs, hash browns, smoked sausage, and omelettes. Add one of Frank's "world famous biscuits," and you're set to start the day off right. Come back for lunch, try the baked or grilled chicken, chicken-fried steak, beef tips, or catfish, and you've made the circuit Southern style. Throw in a tantalizing array of desserts such as lemon icebox pie and peach cobbler, and you'll understand what Southerners miss most when they're far away from home. When Frank Wallace founded this restaurant in 1972, it was nothing more than a simple hot-dog stand. His friend A. L. Latham bought it from him in 1982, expanded the menu, and started featuring those famous biscuits courtesy of a recipe from Jerry Irvin of Hattiesburg, Mississippi. Frank's Restaurant does a brisk catering business, both on and off the premises, with state and local government agencies as well as local schools. They also provide delivery services to downtown locations upon request. For parties of seven or more, reservations are suggested. This is Jackson's most attractive soul-food venue for sit-down dining.

LITTLE ROCK, ARKANSAS

In 1954, the Supreme Court handed down the landmark Brown v. the Board of Education ruling, declaring discrimination in public schools unconstitutional. Three years later, Congress passed the Civil Rights Act of 1957, legislation that created a Civil Rights Commission and a civil rights division within the Justice Department. This was the period in which Rosa Parks, through her refusal to take a back seat in a public bus, helped inspire the Montgomery boycotts. The Reverend Dr. Martin Luther King, Jr. took the national stage, leading the boycotts and organizing the first march on Washington. A month after the enactment of the Civil Rights Bill, nine children sought entrance to Little Rock's Central High School. Arkansas Governor Oral Fibs stood in opposition, and President Dwight D. Eisenhower called out the National Guard to ensure the children's protection. The 101st Airborne escorted these nine children to Central High School and one year later, on May 27, Ernest Green became its first African American graduate. President Eisenhower had removed the National Guard from the school just three weeks earlier. These events in Little Rock were pivotal moments in the history of the nation's Civil Rights movement.

The Arkansas of the late 1950s is vastly different from the Arkansas of today. In 1985, the state's preeminent school of higher education, the University of Arkansas at Fayetteville, hired an African American coach, Noland Richards, to lead a major sports program, and Richardson and his basketball charges rewarded the state's citizens with a national championship in the 1993-94 season. Whereas Arkansas was headed by a governor much opposed to change in the late 1950s, three decades later then Governor Bill Clinton rose to national prominence on the platform of progressive politics and ultimately captured the nation's highest office.

Little Rock has a number of "traditionally black colleges" Arkansas Baptist College, Philander Smith University, and Shorter College. Nearby Pine Bluff is the home of the University of Arkansas at Pine Bluff, originally founded in 1873 by Joseph Carter Corbin as the Branch Normal School.

Little Rock is a proud city with many compelling reasons to visit. The pace is slow compared to its more northern counterparts, but this is more than offset by the city's alluring Southern

MUSIC

EBONY CLUB

Location: 1515 Wright Ave.
Telephone: (501) 372-9850
Clientele: Young/Mature Adult
Format: Blues/R & B
Cover/Minimum: Yes/No
Calendar: Live Entertainment Sun.
Dress: Classy

Comments: The Ebony Club is an ideal venue for blues and vintage R & B. I anticipated an aging neighborhood haunt, but found instead an energetic little place with tiny red, white, and green lights coursing around the room, a dark blue shag carpet covering both the floor and several support beams, and panel mirrors on the walls surrounding a sea of cocktail tables covered with white linen tablecloths. The room is actually much larger than it appears, seating about 250. Dorothy Moore and her Moore Music Orchestra, bedecked in kinte cloth, made it the perfect setting for an evening of music from R & B's golden era. When she sang "Misty Blue," gray-haired men in three-piece suits nodded and smiled, and the ladies in the audience waved their hands high and sang along. The Ebony Club features touring acts monthly. Bluesboy Willie, Willie Clayton, Latimore, and Bobby Rush have been their most recent headliners. The John Craig Band, a local favorite, plays R & B, blues, and jazz most Sundays. Ed Smith has been at the helm of this club since the mid-1970s. Although he laments that he is barely making ends meet, I suspect that he would rather be doing this than anything else. What it amounts to is simple: there aren't many clubs where you can hear touring acts in an intimate setting, and Smith's place is something of an endangered species. When a city loses a club of this genre, old men sit around and ponder the way things used to be.

57

JUANITA'S MEXICAN CAFE & BAR

Location: 1300 S. Main St.
Telephone: (501) 372-1228
Clientele: Young/Mature Adult
Format: Blues/Reggae/Rock
Cover/Minimum: Yes/No
Calendar: Live Entertainment Wed.–Sat.
Dress: Casual/Classy

Comments: Juanita's Mexican Cafe & Bar is Little Rock's top entertainment showcase. First-time visitors will be swept away immediately by the club's character and charm. The first thing that greets customers upon entering is a bin filled with Texas onions, garlic cloves, jalapeno peppers, and lemons. Red booths line one side of the dining room. A passageway leads to the bar and entertainment room on the left. A large stage sits in the corner, canted so that it faces the entire room. Wooden rails divide the room into thirds: one area with cocktail tables along the bar, a sunken area in the center with another set of tables, and a third area against the far wall with both tables and a dance floor. Graffiti covers the far wall. An outdoor patio with long wooden tables and umbrellas provides a comfortable interlude between sessions by the band. During my first visit, I caught a rousing performance by RAS recording stars the Mystic Revealers. Lead singer Billy Mystic and D. J. Soljah captivated the audience with songs from their debut album, "Young Revolutionaries." The music at Juanita's ranges from jazz to reggae to rock & roll. Among the acts that have appeared here are reggae stars Sister Carol, Mikey Dread, and Roots Radies; blues stars Major Handy, Kenny Neal, Duke Robillard, Koko Taylor, and the Kinsey Report; and jazz standouts Hank Crawford and Jimmy McGriff. The club's reggae line-up garnered them recognition as the "Best Reggae Night Club of 1991" by the Mid-America Music Awards. Juanita's consistently has been acknowledged as the best Mexican restaurant in central Arkansas by the *Arkansas Times Magazine*. The menu offers an intriguing array of delights from south of the border, including mesquite-grilled fish and the "Mexican Dinner De San Antonio." And, of course, there are the margaritas! Open daily for lunch and dinner, this is one you won't want to pass up.

DINING

LINDSEY'S BAR-B-QUE

Location: 203 E. 14th St. (North Little Rock, Ark.)
Telephone: (501) 374-5901
Proprietor: Richard & Shirley Lindsey
Dress: Casual/Classy
Menu: Barbecue
Price: Very Modest
Hours: Mon.–Thurs.: 9:30 A.M.–9:30 P.M.;
Fri.–Sat.: 9:30 A.M.–11:30 P.M.

Comments: Lindsey's is an attractive restaurant accented in tan wood paneling and beige brick. Six sets of booths line the far side of the dining room. Four cubicles sit in the center, separated by pine dividers that double as planters. Oil paintings with Mexican, African, and nature themes accent the decor. One wall displays citations from the *Arkansas Times* dating from 1985 to the present. A serving counter and reception room at the entrance accommodate patrons whose schedules are more suited to the take-out menu. Small, large, and jumbo orders of barbecue beef brisket, pork ribs, chicken, and link sausage are the staple here. Lindsey's is also renowned for their fried peach and apple pies, light and fluffy treats that you simply must save room for. Richard Lindsey has been in the barbecue business since the age of 13. He got his start by working for his uncle, Bishop Donnie L. Lindsey, who founded the restaurant in 1955. In 1972, Bishop Lindsey's duties as a leader in the Church of God in Christ (COGIC) and as the city's first African American alderman became so time consuming that he sold the business to his nephew Richard. The younger Lindsey has not only maintained the high standards set by his uncle, but also has taken the business to the forefront among Arkansas caterers. Local, regional, and state agencies are among his top clients. Each Tuesday, Lindsey's provides the catering services for the Mid-Ark Auto Auction, one of the South's largest auto and truck auctions. They also set up a mobile kitchen and cater for the COGIC's semiannual conferences in Memphis each year. Lindsey barbecues his brisket and ribs for eight to twelve hours, depending on the cut. The meat is offset from the fire and slow-cooked over hickory wood. Sons Richard Junior and Greg work side by side with mom and dad. The product of this Ozark family affair is too good to pass up!

LINDSEY'S HOSPITALITY HOUSE

Location: 207 E. 15th St. (North Little Rock, Ark.)
Telephone: (501) 374-5707
Proprietor: Bishop D. L. Lindsey
Dress: Casual / Classy
Menu: Barbecue / Southern
Price: Very Modest
Hours: Mon.–Fri.: 11:00 A.M.–4:00 P.M.

Comments: Lindsey's Hospitality House is both a restaurant and a full-service banquet facility. A small room at the front of the restaurant includes a long display case holding an assortment of delights such as pecan, lemon meringue, and sweet-potato pie. The dining room is attractively decorated in light blue with long wall mirrors and African American folk art throughout. An archway at the rear of the dining room leads to an elegant banquet room in soft pastels, with a mix of cafe and banquet-shaped dining tables and a glass chandelier. The rooms seat 70 and 200 respectively. After a break from the restaurant business of almost two decades, Bishop D. L. Lindsey opened this complex in 1989. The building also includes a religious bookstore operated by his wife Irma and a beauty salon operated by his daughter Donna. Another daughter, DeJuana, and son Donnie Junior co-manage the restaurant. The most-requested items on the menu are beef short ribs, smothered chicken, fresh mixed greens, candied yams, and fried, hot-water cornbread. The cornbread is light but firm, similar in texture and taste to cake. During hunting season, the restaurant also does a thriving business preparing game that customers bring in from the field. They have a long list of patrons who come by to have their venison smoked, for example. The restaurant's banquet room is a local favorite for family and class reunions, wedding receptions, and special events such as the "national conference of black ministers" hosted by President Clinton's 1992 campaign staff. The restaurant also caters for a wide range of civic and public organizations, ranging from the school system to state and municipal arms of government. Lindsey's Hospitality House is yet another of Little Rock's outstanding soul-food restaurants, each of which rates among the best in the Southeast.

SIMS' BAR-B-QUE

Location: 716 W. 33rd St.
Telephone: (501) 372-6868
Proprietor: The Sims Family
Dress: Casual/Classy
Menu: Barbecue
Price: Very Modest
Hours: Mon.–Thurs.: 11:00 A.M.–9:00 P.M.;
Fri.–Sat.: 11:00 A.M.–11:00 P.M.

Comments: Sims' Bar-B-Que is a cozy, attractive restaurant located adjacent to the Greater Center Star Baptist Church. The restaurant's decor is accented by brown cedar panels, white formica tables, and black vinyl chairs. Barbecue beef, pork, and chicken are the most-requested items on the menu. The pork shoulders are cooked from one and a half to two hours, the brisket for about eight hours. The sauce is mustard based. Margaret Sims bakes their sweet-potato pies and an assortment of mouthwatering cakes such as red velvet, Italian cream, and lemon-glazed pound cake. Although the sign out front says the place was founded in 1932 (a painter's error), the late Allen Sims actually founded this landmark establishment in 1942, after having labored in an aluminum plant for a number of years to finance his lifelong dream of owning a restaurant. He nurtured the business for more than 30 years, gaining widespread popularity and respect within the community. In 1976, he retired and leased the restaurant to his nephew Allen Sims II and grandnephew Ronald Settlers. When he died in the early 1980s, he left them the restaurant. The nephews have more than honored the tradition started by their uncle, and the business has, in recent years, expanded to two additional restaurants, one on Geyer Springs Road and another at Barrow Road. As is the case with every restaurant highlighted for Little Rock, Sims' does a thriving business with all segments of the city's population. Catering clients range from area companies to local schools to family reunions. President Bill Clinton ate here on several occasions when he was Arkansas' governor and attorney general. The restaurant frequently has been singled out as central Arkansas' best barbecue shop by the *Arkansas Times*.

DANCING

CLUB CAMEO

Location: 222 E. Washington Ave.
(North Little Rock, Ark.)
Telephone: (501) 372-8814
Clientele: Young Adult
Format: R & B/Hip Hop
Calendar: Dancing Thurs.–Sat.
Cover/Minimum: Yes/No
Dress: Casual/Classy

Comments: Club Cameo is Little Rock's top club for R & B and hip hop. Students from all the neighboring colleges—Philander Smith, the University of Arkansas at Little Rock and Pine Bluff, Arkansas Baptist, and Shorter—consider it one of their favorite stops, and owner J. D. Lipscomb estimates that as much as 45 percent of his club's 600 capacity is made up of this clientele. Pine panels, small walnut-grain formica tables, and red vinyl chairs accentuate the club's decor. A gigantic dance floor in front of the stage is normally crammed with dancers most Thursdays through Saturdays. Lipscomb has owned the club since 1977, starting with only the poolroom next door. He obtained a lease on the entire building in 1978 and opened the club as the 50 Yard Line. In 1991, he changed the name to Club Cameo. During the late 1970s and early 1980s, the club featured numerous touring blues and R & B acts. Of late, the closest thing to live entertainment has been the club's enormously popular Saturday night lip sync contest. Interestingly, Al Green and Johnny Taylor are the most popular artists to imitate. If dancing to the latest R & B chart hits is your pleasure, Club Cameo is the place to go in Little Rock.

EL RANCHO

Location: 1721 S. Scott Street
Telephone: (501) 372-8601
Clientele: Mature Adult
Format: R & B/Jazz/Blues
Calendar: Live Entertainment Tues.– Wed. & Sun.
Cover/Minimum: Yes/No
Dress: Casual/Classy

Comments: El Rancho has the feel of a neighborhood club. Poster art, sombreros, a bull's horn, and a few mirrors are among the items that adorn the brown wood panel walls. The room is rectangular, with three rows of tables lined end to end perpendicular to the band. A dance floor on the far side of the room and a black vinyl-trimmed bar in back round out the decor. The room is spontaneous, very spontaneous. Patrons are as apt to take to the dance floor as they are to engage in call and response with the band. On a particularly inspiring musical note, the bartender is likely to ring a cow bell in exultation. Two local bands, Recovery and the No Name Band, provide a mix of golden-era R & B, blues, and jazz. You'll find as diverse a crowd as any here, from schoolteacher to lawyer to truck driver. The facade is dim and faded, but don't let that mislead you—El Rancho is one of the best places in town to let your hair down and meet residents from throughout the city.

DINING

GRANNY'S KITCHEN

Location: 1019 University Dr.

Telephone: (501) 534-7112

Proprietor: Alfred Austin

Dress: Casual/Classy

Menu: Southern

Price: Very Modest

Hours: Daily: 10:30 A.M.–11:00 P.M. (Summer);
Sun.–Thurs.: 10:30 A.M.–11:00 P.M.,
Fri.–Sat.: 10:00 A.M.–4:00 A.M. (Fall-Spring)

Comments: Granny's Kitchen is an attractive eatery located across the street from the University of Arkansas at Pine Bluff. The building originally housed a fast-food restaurant. The interior resembles the decor in most fast-food franchises, except for a serving line with steaming trays of soulful delights such as fried chicken, pepper steak, candied yams, and mustard and turnip greens. The cooks begin preparing the daily meals at 6:00 A.M. According to owner Alfred Austin, the most-requested dishes are the greens, yams, black-eyed peas, and any entree with gravy on it: usually smothered chicken, steaks, and ribs. The smothered steak, incidentally, is mouth watering. Austin's customers say that they can come here, eat a rib-sticking meal, and be content for the remainder of the day. Austin has been in the food-service business since the early 1970s. After owning a number of limited-menu restaurants, he decided in 1992 that Pine Bluff needed a place where one could go and always get a meal like grandmother used to make, piping hot vegetables and entrees that made you feel at home when traveling or eating out. The restaurant operates later on Friday and Saturday nights during the school year to accommodate the appetites of nearby university students. From fall to spring, they run a short-order menu after 9:00 P.M. that is available until 4:00 A.M. Alfred Austin's wife Margaret Eleanor works full-time at the restaurant. Daughter Emily puts in an afternoon's work after her high-school studies. Another daughter, Detria, helps out during the summer between pre-med studies at Atlanta's Spelman College. This is down-home cooking at its finest.

64

DANCING

PJ'S DISCO

Location: 2411 University Dr.
Telephone: (501) 534-9864
Clientele: Young Adult
Format: R & B/Blues/Jazz
Calendar: Live Entertainment Varies; Dancing Fri.–Sat.
Cover/Minimum: Yes/No
Dress: Casual

Comments: PJ's has been described by many as the most beautiful club in the South. The closer one gets to Arkansas, the more insistent patrons become, asserting that it is, at the very least, one of the top ten clubs in the country. "After all, how many clubs feature two indoor swimming pools?" Needless to say, I couldn't wait to lay eyes on this place. From the outside, the club resembles a flying saucer rimmed in thin beams of red neon. Inside, it's simply stunning. The atrium is alive with potted plants. A passageway to the right leads to the main entertainment room, an elegant space lined with oak-trimmed mirrors, rows of V-shaped tubing suspended from the ceiling that pulsate with tiny flecks of light, white leather chairs, and white linen-clad tables. The two hardwood dance floors elevated one above the other get plenty of use. An alcove near the rear leads to an indoor patio with a large swimming pool flanked by potted ferns and white wrought-iron chairs. A room on the far side, nestled behind white drapes, conceals a full-service beauty salon. Should you have turned left upon entering the building, you would have found a lounge decorated with brown leather chairs and a hardwood bar, and yet another room, the sports bar, replete with billiard tables and video monitors. The club was founded in 1971 by James R. Seawood. Then it was part of the Collegiate Plaza, nestled in the middle of soybean and cotton fields. Perry Johnson bought the property in the late 1970s and expanded it, little by little, until it reached its current configuration in 1987. The club now accommodates 700 patrons in a sprawling seven-acre complex. PJ's has experimented with several formats in recent years, but is returning to an R & B, blues, and jazz mix. Bobby "Blue" Bland, Millie Jackson, and Bobby Rush are among the most recent acts that have headlined. Stop by, and you'll understand why so many Arkansas natives rave about this spectacular facility.

65

MEMPHIS, TENNESSEE

One of the founding fathers of Memphis was Andrew Jackson who was later to become the United States' seventh president. After he and two partners bought huge parcels of land on the banks of the Mississippi and Wolf Rivers in the 1780s, they negotiated a treaty with the Chickasaw Indians and laid the foundation for what was to grow into one of the jewel cities of the South.

Two events that have had a profound effect on the character of American life took place here. In 1968, the Reverend Dr. Martin Luther King, Jr., came to the city to show support for the striking Memphis sanitation workers. It was during this visit that he was assassinated while standing on the balcony of the Lorraine Motel. This single moment crystallized the Civil Rights movement in the United States. It gave added momentum to the struggle, elevated the consciousness of all Americans, and assured Dr. King an immortal place worldwide as a champion of freedom.

The second event occurred a century earlier when William Christopher Handy reached down into the depths of his soul, tapped into the trials and tribulations of "Negro folk," and came up with a rhythm that is uniquely American: the blues. Handy's presence is felt throughout Memphis, but nowhere more so than on Beale Street.

Much has been said and written about this legendary thoroughfare. While it is well known that jug bands and blues artists gave life to this gathering place, Beale Street was more than the music it nourished. It was the heart of the city's African American community, a place where African American entrepreneurs, professionals, and just plain ordinary folk struggled to survive. During the early 1930s, Robert Church, Sr., a man said to be the first African American millionaire, amassed a fortune as an entrepreneur and real estate investor on Beale Street. His son, Robert Junior, carried on his father's legacy and became a well known and powerful political figure.

Memphis is rich in American lore and music history. From the "historically black college" Lemoyne-Owens University to the home of Elvis Presley to the Civil Rights Museum, there is much to see and much to appreciate in this beautiful city.

MUSIC

B. B. KING'S BLUES CLUB

Location: 143 Beale St.
Telephone: (901) 524-KING
Clientele: Young/Mature Adult
Format: Memphis Music (R & B)/Blues
Calendar: Live Entertainment & Dancing Nightly
Cover/Minimum: Yes/No
Dress: Classy

Comments: B. B. King's Blues Club is a perfect venue for the blues and R & B oldies. I adopted it as one of my favorite clubs the minute I walked in the door. King's is a throwback to times of old, when house parties reigned supreme. That's what you get every evening: patrons throng to the dance floor or engage in high-spirited audience response whenever the band hits an irresistable groove. A number of photos adorn the walls, including one of "Blues Boy" B. B. King with Elvis Presley, as well as shots of Sam and Dave, Al Green, Muddy Waters, and Johnny Taylor. The King B's, featuring Ruby Wilson, rock the house seven nights a week. Rarekas Bonds, one of Ruby's "kids," may come in and dance for you—he's the boy who tumbled across the screen in the Tom Cruise movie *The Firm*. B. B. King performs about twice each year. Other national acts have included blues stars Clarence "Gatemouth" Brown, the late Albert Collins, Buddy Guy, and Irma Thomas. Paul McCartney's band, Aerosmith, and Eric Clapton have sat in. B. B. King's also puts on special tributes. One of the most popular was a Stax Records revue that included a tribute to the late, great R & B star, Otis Redding, and featured his grandson Otis Redding III, Booker T. and the MG's, Sam Moore, the Memphis Horns, and Eddie Floyd. The main dining room forms a semicircle around the dance floor and stage. An alcove on the second floor also affords comfortable dining while allowing a panoramic view of the stage. The menu ranges from "King Steak, a ribeye smothered with Sauteed Onions, Mushrooms, Peppers, and covered with Mozzarella Cheese" to the grilled or deep-fried catfish dinner. One of the most-requested desserts is the strawberry icebox pie. The red beans and rice are as good as you'll find anywhere outside of New Orleans. Although the club seats 400, reservations are recommended. The restaurant serves lunch from 11:30 A.M.

BLUES CITY CAFE

Location: 138 Beale St.
Telephone: (901) 526-3637
Clientele: Young/Mature Adult
Format: Blues/R & B/Jazz
Calendar: Live Entertainment Nightly
Cover/Minimum: Yes/No
Dress: Casual/Classy

Comments: Blues City Cafe has been one of the most happening clubs on Beale Street since it opened in March 1991. In fact, it's the place where Beale Street musicians and club employees go for late-night dining and more blues. The club features an attractive dining room on one side and a lounge on the other. The music of choice is blues, of course, and Memphis-flavored R & B. Albert King, Steve Winwood, John Hammond, Mose Allison, Joe Walsh, and Richie Havens are just some of the national touring acts that have performed here. Preston Shannon, a Bullseye Blues recording artist, is the featured act. From November to February, the club principally features regional acts, while bookings in the spring and summer frequently showcase nationally renowned artists. The Memphis Horns had the release party here for their first solo album, "Flame Out." Blues City Cafe also has an outstanding menu that includes barbecue ribs, frog legs, and their two most popular entrees, quail and steak. In 1992, *Vogue* magazine described the steak cooked by chef B. Lewis Mack, Sr., as "the best in the world." This is one Memphis establishment that is carrying on the Beale Street tradition in grand fashion.

GREEN'S LOUNGE

Location: 2090 East Person Ave.

Telephone: (901) 274-9802

Clientele: Mature Adult

Format: Blues

Calendar: Live Entertainment Fri.–Sat.

Cover/Minimum: Yes/No

Dress: Casual/Classy

Comments: Rose Green operated this traditional blues juke joint for more than 20 years. In January 1994, she turned the club over to Betty Suggs, who also knows her way around the blues circuit, having owned a number of places in Memphis as well as the Silver Slipper in Clarksdale, Mississippi. Green's is short on pomp and circumstance but heavy, oh so heavy, on low-down, hard-hitting blues, mostly Delta blues. By day, the club takes on the characteristics of an old neighborhood bar. Elderly men play cards, usually Spades or Bid Whist. The jukebox belts out Little Milton tunes, "Struggling Lady" and "Catch You On The Way Back Down." On weekends, the club undergoes a transformation, becoming something resembling the juke joint recreated in Steven Spielberg's *The Color Purple*, alive and festive. The Fieldstones rock the house, as they have done for more than two decades, belting out Delta blues flavored by Memphis tradition. Big Joe and the Dynaflows surprised the folks at Green's Lounge recently by dropping in to "jump" the house while in town for an engagement at B. B. King's. Regular patrons at Green's Lounge range from old faithfuls who have lived in the neighborhood for years, dressed in bell-bottom pants or plaids, to folks who drive up in limousines, sporting the latest fashions in evening wear. Rich or poor, white or black, they all have one thing in common. They want to hear and experience the blues as it was sung and performed at juke joints throughout the Delta and in Memphis by legendary blues artists. Rose Green has been coaxed out of retirement to bring back another feature of the club from years past, down-home cooking that yields soulful staples such as chitterlings, ham hocks, turnips, and black-eyed peas. If you are a diehard blues connoisseur, your stay in Memphis won't be complete without stepping back in time and jamming at Green's Lounge.

69

HUEY'S

Location: 1927 Madison Ave.
Telephone: (901) 727-4372
Clientele: Young/Mature Adult
Format: Memphis Music (R & B)/Blues/Jazz
Calendar: Live Entertainment Sun.
Cover/Minimum: Yes/No
Dress: Classy

Comments: In a city where such offerings are limited, Huey's has provided a jazz venue for more than 18 years. Still, it owes its first allegiance to the blues. The list of blues artists who have either headlined here or sat in with the house band is enormous. "Big Joe" Williams held his last performance here. Matt "Guitar" Murphy, George Thorogood, Son Seals, and Koko Taylor have also put on memorable performances. One of the really special times to catch a show at Huey's is during the week of the annual Handy Awards, an event that honors the top blues artists of the past year and key individuals responsible for keeping blues alive in America. The Midtown Jazzmobile has been the featured jazz act at Huey's since the mid-1970s, although the cast of musicians has changed somewhat over the years. Jim Spake plays a mean saxophone (baritone, tenor, and soprano) and is one of the best reasons to catch their act. This group of talented Memphis musicians plays everything from bebop to hard bop to contemporary. The jazz show starts at 4:00 P.M.; however, get there by 3:30 for a good seat. The club undergoes a metamorphosis as the evening goes on and the jazz crowd gives way to the blues crowd. The blues gets underway at 9:00 P.M. Again, getting there a half hour early improves your chance of getting a good seat, the closer to the band, the better. While the club normally holds about 120, on some Sundays that number swells to almost 200. Another reason to check Huey's out is their menu of continental cuisine, hamburgers (voted the city's best for ten years running), and assorted sandwiches. The restaurant, open daily at 11:00 A.M. for lunch and dinner, serves until around 3:00 A.M. Huey's has two other locations: Huey's II at 2858 Hickory Hill Road in southeast Memphis and Huey's III at 1771 North Germantown in the Cordova suburb, an area on the city's northeast side.

KING'S PALACE CAFE

Location: 162 Beale St.
Telephone: (901) 521-1851
Clientele: Mature Adult
Format: Blues/Memphis Music (R & B)
Calendar: Live Entertainment
& Dancing Nightly (Mar.–Sept.)
Cover/Minimum: Yes/No
Dress: Classy

Comments: King's Palace Cafe, opened in 1989, is a sedate blues and R & B supper club most popular among older Memphis residents and tourists. The music is toned down, the lights are low, and the atmosphere is rather chic as Beale Street establishments go. While many clubs in the celebrated neighborhood offer the atmosphere of a frolicking dance party, patrons of King's Palace Cafe are more interested in a venue where they can sit back and relax, feast on a good meal, and enjoy the music. Jazz occasionally is featured here, the most memorable act being Maynard Ferguson in 1991. The primary focus, however, is blues and R & B. The house band, the Charlie Wood Trio, serves up a little bit of jazz and blues and a lot of Memphis music. The music generally runs from 7:00 P.M to 11:00 P.M. The club's peak months are mid-March through Labor Day weekend. During the off-season, you can expect to see a show each Friday and Saturday evening. The menu includes pasta dishes, Cajun cuisine, and steaks.

71

MALLARD'S BAR & GRILL

Location: 114 Union Ave.
Telephone: (901) 529-4183
Clientele: Young/Mature Adult
Format: Blues
Calendar: Live Entertainment Varies
Cover/Minimum: Yes/No
Dress: Classy

Comments: The posh and elegant Mallard's Bar & Grill is in the historic Peabody Hotel. Booker T. Laury, Ruby Wilson, and Jason D. Williams were regularly featured during the late 1980s and early 1990s. The list of people who have sat in include Memphis Slim, Isaac Hayes, and Phineas Newborn, Jr. The bar recently showcased a jazz supper club format. Fred Ford and the Honeymoon Garner Trio were featured over the Christmas holiday, playing a range of jazz from contemporary to bebop. They also regaled their audience with anecdotes about their experiences playing Beale Street during the late 1930s and 1940s. The celebrity wall on the far side of the room reads like a who's who of entertainment: Calvin Lockhart, Tom Cruise, Lou Rawls, Patti La Belle, Minnie Pearl, Al Hirt, and the Four Tops, just to name a few. Whether you stop in for a show or just for a leisurely cocktail, you have to visit the Peabody and Mallard's and sample a bit of Memphis history.

MARMALADE RESTAURANT & LOUNGE

Location: 153 E. Calhoun St.
Telephone: (901) 522-8800
Clientele: Young / Mature Adult
Format: Jazz / Blues / R & B
Calendar: Live Entertainment Fri.–Sun.
Cover/Minimum: Yes / No
Dress: Casual / Classy

Comments: During the early 1980s, there were few opportunities for African American performers to showcase their talents in Memphis. The Beale Street renovation was still a few years off. But L. B. Smith, a longtime teacher in the Memphis public schools, and his wife Mae, a retiree from the postal system, harbored a dream of owning a restaurant and lounge. After extensive research into the Memphis entertainment market, they opened Marmalade in 1982. The result was an immediate success. The club is in an attractive, spacious building adjacent to two Memphis landmarks: the Civil Rights Museum (Lorraine Motel), and the office of the *Tri-State Defender*, the city's only African American-owned newspaper. The Duncan Sisters, Ruby Wilson, and the Smiths' son Audi were among the club's first headliners. It also features top regional acts such as Joyce Cobb, Willie Covington, and Chic and Melinda Rogers. The club has a softly lit dining room, a lounge, a TV room, and a private banquet area. In addition to fine entertainment, Marmalade offers an outstanding menu of Southern cuisine. The house specialty is seafood gumbo. Many find the grilled pork chops irresistible. De Barge, Arthur Prysock, and Maurice White (Earth, Wind and Fire) are but a few of the celebrities who have visited. Stop by and enjoy the entertainment, the food, and Mae Smith's gracious Southern hospitality.

MR. HANDY'S BLUES HALL

Location: 174 Beale St.
Telephone: (901) 528-0150
Clientele: Young/Mature Adult
Format: Blues
Calendar: Live Entertainment Varies
Cover/Minimum: Yes/No
Dress: Casual/Classy

Comments: Mr. Handy's Blues Hall is adjacent to Rum Boogie Cafe. In fact, a door donated by the Memphis Blues Society adjoins them. This door says much about the venue at Blues Hall— it's adorned with covers from program booklets for the annual Handy Awards. The club's design is reminiscent of an authentic old blues honky-tonk. Intimate and small, it's like the mythical smoked-filled room where blues acts of yesteryear performed until the wee hours and the patrons danced the night away. Adorning the walls are old portraits of Beale Street residents, dressed in the high fashions typical there during the early 1930s. Delta blues is the music of choice here. Patrons often spend an evening traversing back and forth between the party at Rum Boogie's and the down-home ambience of Blues Hall. One cover gains admission to both.

74

NEW CLUB PARADISE

Location: 645 Georgia Ave.
Telephone: (901) 947-7144
Clientele: Young/Mature Adult
Format: Blues/R & B
Calendar: Live Entertainment Varies
Cover/Minimum: Yes/No
Dress: Casual/Classy

Comments: The late "Sunbeam" Andrew Mitchell was both a musician and an entrepreneur. He was at the core of African American life in Memphis during the 1960s. Under the helm of Mitchell, Club Paradise set the standard for blues, jazz, and R & B in the region at a time when no other entertainment venues existed for African Americans there. Braxton recalls that during peak periods Club Paradise drew standing-room-only crowds five nights a week. This was partly attributed to a list of acts that virtually chronicles the evolution of blues, jazz, and R & B in the United States; performers included the Count Basie Band, Cab Calloway, Muddy Waters, Howlin' Wolf, James Brown, Jackie Wilson, and Etta James. Paul Jordan took over the club and renamed it New Club Paradise in 1985. He is fiercely dedicated to keeping the legacy of this historic establishment alive. The management has spent more than $1 million on renovations to achieve that objective. The club's plain facade completely conceals the sleek and attractive decor inside. Since its reopening, the club has been host to acts such as Freddie Jackson, Melba Moore, Denise LaSalle, Tyronne Davis, and the O'Jays. Jordan hopes to re-establish New Club Paradise as a top entertainment center for Memphis residents and visitors. Give them a call when you're visiting the area to see what's on their calendar.

75

THE NORTH END

Location: 346 N. Main St.
Telephone: (901) 526-0319
Clientele: Young/Mature Adult
Format: Jazz/Blues
Calendar: Live Entertainment Wed., Fri.–Sun.
Cover/Minimum: Yes/No
Dress: Casual/Classy

Comments: The North End is a large and airy establishment located near the Pyramid Complex in the downtown area. It has the feel of a college bistro, a description born out by North End's immense popularity among Memphis State students and young Memphis professionals. North End has high ceilings and a decor accentuated by an interesting assortment of memorabilia on the walls such as old Coca-Cola and gas-station signs. The club seats 120, while the patio accommodates another 100 patrons. On Wednesdays, Rico's Band performs an eclectic blend of music that ranges from bluegrass to traditional jazz. The Wilson Reid Band plays contemporary country music each Saturday night. Sid Selvidge packs the house with Delta blues each Friday, while Jungle Dust plays fusion jazz on Sundays. For most shows, come about 9:30 P.M. and get your choice of seats for the first set of the evening at 10:00 P.M. There are three sets with each running about 45 minutes. While most patrons come to hear jazz and blues, many just come for North End's cuisine, a menu that includes the best marinated chicken sandwich in town and a hot-fudge concoction topped with French vanilla ice cream and whipped cream that is something to die for. The restaurant is open daily for lunch and dinner. North End also offers the largest imported beer selection in the city. Owner Jake Schorr is a director of the Memphis Queen Lines and also owns a fleet of horse-drawn carriages. His diverse business interests translate into a windfall for patrons of the North End: they can hear some outstanding local blues and jazz acts, have a great meal, arrange a tour of the city by carriage, and set up a riverboat cruise on one of the Memphis Queen Line's blues excursions to Tunica, Mississippi, all in one stop.

RUM BOOGIE CAFE

Location: 182 Beale St.
Telephone: (901) 528-0150
Clientele: Young/Mature Adult
Format: Blues/Memphis Music (R & B)
Calendar: Live Entertainment
& Dancing Nightly
Cover/Minimum: Yes/No
Dress: Casual/Classy

Comments: The Rum Boogie Cafe has been one of the most popular clubs on Beale Street since it opened in 1984. Like many establishments in the neighborhood, the decor is alive with graffiti and guitars autographed by music legends who have played here including Albert Collins, Bo Didley, Willie Dixon, Billy Gibbons of ZZ Top, and the late Stevie Ray Vaughan. The main room has a stage, a dance floor, and ample seating. A spiral staircase leads to the second-floor alcove where you can dine as well as look down on the stage. The neon sign that hangs above the stage was once the marquis for the Stax Recording Studio. Don McMinn and the Rum Boogie Band held court at Rum Boogie's for more than nine years until 1994, when McMinn left to go on tour and record. The new house band is Stone Blue featuring local favorite James Govan. In addition to the fantastic entertainment that is a staple, Rum Boogie Cafe boasts a menu that includes a seafood gumbo rated tops in the city four years running by the annual Cajun Crawfish & Gumbo Festival held in April. The cafe is open for lunch and dinner daily. This is one of Beale Street's feature attractions. Don't miss an opportunity to take in some hot blues and R & B here while visiting Memphis.

WILLIE MITCHELL'S RHYTHM & BLUES CLUB

Location: 326 Beale St.
Telephone: (901) 523-7444
Clientele: Young/Mature Adult
Format: Blues/R & B
Calendar: Live Entertainment Fri.–Sun.
Cover/Minimum: Yes/No
Dress: Casual/Classy

Comments: Willie Mitchell's Rhythm & Blues Club is one of the newest additions to the Beale Street entertainment scene. Gold and platinum albums of gospel-and-R & B star Al Green line the walls at the entrance, a testament to the creative achievements of the club's namesake, composer and arranger Willie Mitchell. A hardwood bar inlaid with green-and-white tile and a large hardwood dance floor make up the first room. A second room, lined with scores of photos depicting legendary R & B stars, is used as a meeting and conference room. An outdoor patio decorated with white wrought-iron patio furniture also is used as an entertainment venue. The club's capacity is 250. Bobby Rush and the Hi Rhythm Band with Teenie Hodges and the Hodges Brothers were the first touring acts to play the club. Local star Preston Shannon and the Preston Shannon Band is regularly featured. Trumpeter and composer Willie Mitchell played the room in July 1994, his first performance in the United States in 25 years. The club intends to feature touring acts monthly as well as appearances by Mitchell. Local promoter Bob Winbush puts on a talent search, "Stairway to the Stars," each Wednesday night. Yvonne Mitchell founded the club in March 1994. She and her sister Lorraine co-managed Ann Peebles for a number of years. Yvonne Mitchell also has been something of a "lady Friday" for Royal Record Studios (formerly Hi Records) since the early 1970s, helping her father Willie Mitchell in a wide range of duties. Willie Mitchell's Rhythm & Blues Club is very much the family affair with the two sisters' kids, Archie, Donna, and Lawrence actively involved in the business. The menu includes entrees such as roast prime rib, fried shrimp, grilled smothered chicken, red beans and rice, and a catch of the day. Homemade cobblers and apple, coconut, and pecan pies round out their dessert selections. The restaurant is open for lunch and dinner from 1:30 P.M.

DINING

THE BAR-B-QUE SHOP

Location: 1782 Madison Ave.
Telephone: (901) 272-1277
Proprietor: Frank Vernon
Dress: Casual/Classy
Menu: Barbecue
Price: Modest
Hours: Mon.–Thurs.: 11:00 A.M.–10:00 P.M.;
Fri.–Sat.: 11:00 A.M.–11:00 P.M.

Comments: Frank Vernon worked at UPS for 13 years and often would stop by Brady & Lil's for some of their famous barbecue and swap tales with the owner, Brady P. Vinson. During one of those visits, Vinson indicated that he was considering retiring and wanted to know whether Vernon was serious about getting into the business. After some soul searching and deliberation with his wife Hazel, Vernon accepted the opportunity. They negotiated a purchase price and, more importantly, Vinson offered to stay on to show Vernon the ropes, sharing his recipes and other important barbecue secrets. Vernon took this fateful step in 1978. In 1987, he changed the name of the place to The Bar-B-Que Shop to establish more firmly his own identity in the community. He has more than carried on the tradition of this family restaurant, however. He credits his wife and the late Brady Vinson as being the keys to his success. Vernon's son Eric comes in to help in the kitchen between his studies at Memphis State University. Frank Vernon says that his method of barbecuing is unique. His sauce (made from scratch with a tomato-paste base) is so good that he sells it to customers by the quart—he has even considered mass-marketing it. Vernon slow-cooks his meat over charcoal with oak and hickory logs, placing a foil over the ribs and Boston butt shoulders to retain their juices. The result is some of the most incredible ribs you'll ever have. The *New York Times*, *People* magazine, and the local *Memphis Commercial Appeal* heartily agree. Vernon provides catering services to many businesses in the city, including Federal Express, Holiday Inn, and Hewlett-Packard. B. B. King, Cybil Shepherd, and Bobby "Blue" Bland are but a few of the celebrities who have stopped in to sample the delights.

COZY CORNER

Location: 745 North Pkwy.
Telephone: (901) 527-9158
Proprietor: Raymond Robinson, Jr.
Dress: Casual
Menu: Soul Food
Price: Modest
Hours: Tues.–Sat.: 10:30 A.M.–7:00 P.M.

Comments: Raymond Robinson, Sr., who had made a living making Titan missiles for Martin Marietta, returned to Memphis in 1966 in search of business opportunities. In 1976, he took the entrepreneurial plunge and achieved enormous success. His Cozy Corner barbecue place has evolved into a family affair that ranks among the city's best. Hostess Neval Robinson, Raymond Senior's mother, gives the restaurant a down-home feel. She'll welcome you with a warm smile and ensure that you are comfortable, while simultaneously tending to her great-grandchildren who sometimes drop by to do their homework. Raymond Junior now runs the business while his dad oversees and passes on his expertise. Barbecue pork, beef, Cornish hen, and turkey are the specialties. While the ribs are most popular, smoked turkeys are big around the Christmas holidays. In December 1993, patrons walked out carrying smoked turkeys by the armloads—more than 250 on the weekend before Christmas! One of the keys to the delicious flavor of Cozy Corner ribs is the dry rub, which Raymond Senior sprinkles on after he has trimmed away excess fat. The rub, which is made entirely of spices, penetrates the meat by way of its natural juices. Slow- cooking the ribs for two to three hours is the final step. The result is superb. Throwing down some delicious ribs is but one of the pleasures of a meal at Cozy Corner. Raymond Senior can regale you for hours on end with stories about Memphis life and lore. James Alexander of the Bar-Kays R & B group joined us at our booth for an engaging conversation. Entertainers and celebrities seem to be drawn to this establishment. Cybil Shepherd stopped by and filmed a scene from her movie *Our Town* right on the premises. A scene from *Coming From Africa* also was filmed here. This is one of those places where eating is just half the fun. Southern hospitality and good old-fashioned conversation are the added attractions.

ESTHER'S ON THE SQUARE

Location: 111 S. Court St.
Telephone: (901) 527-9777/522-8574
Proprietor: Esther Merriweather
Dress: Casual/Classy
Menu: Soul Food
Price: Modest
Hours: Daily: 6:00 A.M.–10:00 P.M.

Comments: Esther's is a cozy restaurant and lounge in the heart of downtown Memphis. Although Esther Merriweather established her place in 1992, she has been in the business since 1951, her first restaurant being Junior's Lunch Room on Front Street. Like many of the South's fine soul-food restaurants, hers is a family affair, and her daughter Carol Jones, son Cedric Senior, and grandson Cedric Junior are all key players in the business. Merriweather says that her most-requested dishes are the chitterlings, barbecue, and catfish fillets. I had a great meal of pork shoulder, steamed cabbage, and baked beans. You'll also want to try their delicious desserts such as peach cobbler, white chocolate cheesecake, and sweet-potato pie. Esther's features a buffet-style as well as a sit-down menu. The tri-level restaurant also features a patio for dining on balmy summer evenings. The downstairs lounge showcases live entertainment each weekend, running the gamut of jazz, R & B, blues, and reggae. T. J. and L'Entourage, a local jazz group, was the feature act during Christmas and New Year's 1993. You'll definitely enjoy a breakfast, lunch, or dinner at this attractive establishment. It's also a great choice for a weekend evening of entertainment.

FOURWAY GRILL

Location: 998 Mississippi Blvd.
Telephone: (901) 775-2351/9384
Proprietor: Irene Cleaves
Dress: Casual
Menu: Soul Food
Price: Very Modest
Hours: Daily: 7:00 A.M.–11:00 P.M.

Comments: The Fourway Grill is one of Memphis's most-celebrated soul-food restaurants, widely chronicled in official tour guides and in a number of books about the city's history and cuisine. It is also one of those landmark institutions that has managed to survive more than half a century. Irene Cleaves and her late husband Clint founded the restaurant in 1946. It is sparse on decor, but heavy on tradition, enjoying a long list of customers whose allegiance spans generations. The list includes a number of honored guests such as the Reverend Dr. Martin Luther King, Jr., the Reverend Jesse Jackson, Nat King Cole, Alex Haley, "Sugar Ray" Robinson, Gladys Knight and the Pips, and Lionel Hampton. If these walls could talk, what a story they could tell! The booths and tables are worn, but what is prepared and delivered when you order is just as the citizens of Memphis proudly proclaim: traditional soul food prepared in the down-home fashion, and plenty of it! I enjoyed a feast of Southern fried chicken, turnip greens, and northern beans. Other popular items from the menu include chitterlings, baked beef spareribs, ham hocks, and fried catfish. The stewed apples and yam patties are fantastic. When you enter the Fourway Grill, you'll get both an incredible meal and a big slice of American history.

JIM NEELY'S INTERSTATE BAR-B-QUE

Location: 2265 S. 3rd St.
Telephone: (901) 775-2304
Proprietor: Jim Neely
Dress: Casual/Classy
Menu: Barbecue
Price: Modest
Hours: Mon.–Thurs.: 11:00 A.M.–11:00 P.M.;
Fri.–Sat.: 11:00 A.M.–2:00 A.M.; Sun.: 12:00 P.M.–10:00 P.M.

Comments: While traveling throughout the South on insurance business during the late 1970s, barbecue lover Jim Neely began to think about devoting more time to entrepreneurial pursuits. He decided to convert a recently acquired building into a barbecue restaurant and launched his new business in March 1980. It was an immediate and resounding success. Neely takes great satisfaction in putting out a quality product. One of the key elements to his barbecue's popularity is the pit. It's Neely's own design, and there are only six in existence. (Jim Neely has two, and his two nephews of Neely's Barbecue have two each.) I won't reveal the design of these pits, but I will say that the fire is offset from the meat. Other keys include the use of a select cut of brisket (away from the fat or muscle) and ribs that are exclusively "three and down." Neely only uses corn-fed Midwestern hogs. The slow-cooking process, ranging from three and a half hours for ribs to fifteen hours for pork brisket, locks in the flavor that is uniquely Jim Neely's. He prepares 60 quarts of sauce four times daily. His sauce, with a tomato base of 33 1/2 percent solids, features a special blend of herbs and spices. Patrons are attracted to Neely's Interstate Bar-B-Que from all corners of Memphis society and from all parts of the country. Over the years, Neely's has received an avalanche of favorable publicity. *People* magazine, for example, published the results of a national survey in 1989 rating Neely's second in the country behind the legendary Arthur Bryant's Rib House of Kansas City, Missouri. George Carlin, Susan Sarandon, Betty Shabazz, and Rufus Thomas are among the legions of celebrities who have dropped in for Neely's special fare. This restaurant should definitely be included among your dining choices when visiting the city.

MELANIE'S & THE LEACH FAMILY RESTAURANT

Location: 1070 N. Watkins St./694 Madison St.
Telephone: (901) 278-0751/521-0867
Proprietor: Jimmie Mae Cotton-Leach and the Leach Family
Dress: Casual
Menu: Soul Food
Price: Modest
Hours: Mon.–Sat.: 11:00 A.M.–6:00 P.M.

Comments: Jimmie Mae Cotton-Leach has always enjoyed cooking and collecting recipes, and she has cooked for her church most of her life. When visiting evangelists came to town in the 1960s, the Leach family housed and fed them, and on Sundays, all the neighbors would come over to eat. The idea of opening a family restaurant came as an inspiration. Their first establishment, Melanie's, is in an old neighborhood in what is called the "midtown area." The mid-town restaurant has a serving line, but is primarily geared towards take-out orders. The tiny eatery seats about 30 in small booths adorned with blue-and-white tablecloths. The most-requested entrees are fried catfish, served only on Fridays, and fried chicken, served Wednesdays and Saturdays. Both are cooked to a golden brown using special seasonings and spices developed by Mrs. Cotton-Leach. The secret to her chitterlings is that she pot-boils them, washes them again, and then adds yet another of her special seasonings. Other items from the menu include greens, ham hocks, and yams. The restaurant is also well known for delicious lemon cake, peach cobbler, and banana pudding. Melanie's caters for church gatherings, weddings, and local business events. Their cakes are so popular that the Leach family was able to sponsor bake sales to help lay the foundation for their church, True Gospel Church of God and Christ. They give additional support to the local community by providing meals on request to the Greater Movement Homeless Shelter and the Salvation Army. The family also operates the Leach Family Restaurant at 694 Madison Street, run by Jimmie Mae's son Michael. The Leach Family Restaurant is the more attractive of their two establishments and can accommodate twice the number of customers as Melanie's can. Here sit-down dining is the norm. Whichever location you visit is an excellent choice for down-home cooking.

NEELY'S BAR-B-QUE

Location: 670 Jefferson Blvd.
Telephone: (901) 521-9798
Proprietor: Patrick and Tony Neely
Dress: Casual/Classy
Menu: Barbecue
Price: Modest
Hours: Mon.–Thurs.:
10:30 A.M.–9:00 P.M.; Fri.–Sat.: 10:30 A.M.–11:00 P.M.

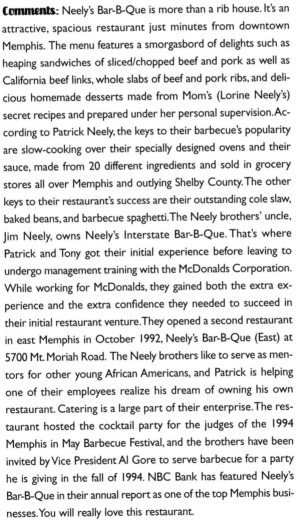

Comments: Neely's Bar-B-Que is more than a rib house. It's an attractive, spacious restaurant just minutes from downtown Memphis. The menu features a smorgasbord of delights such as heaping sandwiches of sliced/chopped beef and pork as well as California beef links, whole slabs of beef and pork ribs, and delicious homemade desserts made from Mom's (Lorine Neely's) secret recipes and prepared under her personal supervision. According to Patrick Neely, the keys to their barbecue's popularity are slow-cooking over their specially designed ovens and their sauce, made from 20 different ingredients and sold in grocery stores all over Memphis and outlying Shelby County. The other keys to their restaurant's success are their outstanding cole slaw, baked beans, and barbecue spaghetti. The Neely brothers' uncle, Jim Neely, owns Neely's Interstate Bar-B-Que. That's where Patrick and Tony got their initial experience before leaving to undergo management training with the McDonalds Corporation. While working for McDonalds, they gained both the extra experience and the extra confidence they needed to succeed in their initial restaurant venture. They opened a second restaurant in east Memphis in October 1992, Neely's Bar-B-Que (East) at 5700 Mt. Moriah Road. The Neely brothers like to serve as mentors for other young African Americans, and Patrick is helping one of their employees realize his dream of owning his own restaurant. Catering is a large part of their enterprise. The restaurant hosted the cocktail party for the judges of the 1994 Memphis in May Barbecue Festival, and the brothers have been invited by Vice President Al Gore to serve barbecue for a party he is giving in the fall of 1994. NBC Bank has featured Neely's Bar-B-Que in their annual report as one of the top Memphis businesses. You will really love this restaurant.

DANCING

THE MANSION

Location: 1397 Central Ave.
Telephone: (901) 722-8877
Clientele: Young/Mature Adult
Format: Top 40/R & B/House
Calendar: Dancing Wed.–Sat.
Cover/Minimum: Yes/No
Dress: Classy

Comments: The Mansion is one of the most innovative and unique concepts for a dance club that you will find anywhere in the South. Imagine dancing the night away in an old Southern mansion, restored to its original splendor and equipped with the latest technology in club lighting and audiovisual effects. From its regal sitting rooms on the first floor to its spacious dance floor in the cellar, the Mansion excites and entertains. Originally constructed by the Snowden family in 1895 as a single-family dwelling, this historic landmark had seen several attempts at commercial use over the years, including a restaurant, but lay in a state of disrepair and neglect until 1990. That's when the current owners undertook a meticulous $1 million plus renovation. Almost two years later, having restored the house to its original condition, they opened the doors as the Castle Night Club. Paul Mattila then took over, tinkered with the format to fine-tune it, and reopened in the fall of 1993 as the Mansion. The final result is delightful. Magic Johnson, singer Freddie Jackson, and NBA star Anfernee Hardaway are but a few of the celebrities who have dropped in for an evening. The Mansion is a must see!

ROBB'S

Location: 2649 N. Hollywood St.
Telephone: (901) 353-9000
Clientele: Young/Mature Adult
Format: R & B/House/Hip Hop
Calendar: Live Entertainment
Bimonthly; Dancing Wed.–Sun.
Cover/Minimum: Yes/No
Dress: Casual/Classy

Comments: Located in the Sky Lake Shopping Center in the Frayser section of town, Robb's is one of the most popular dance establishments in Memphis. This very large club is filled to its capacity of 501 on most weekends. It is illuminated by soft neon lights and television monitors, and the dance floor is surrounded by high tables and high-backed chairs. According to manager Ira Lyons, the club was previously located in the Raleigh area but was destroyed in a fire. They've been at their Frayser location since October 1992. Some of the acts that have appeared here include the Bar Kays, Cameo, Luther Campbell, and Naughty by Nature. Visiting celebrities such as basketball stars Anfernee Hardaway, Scottie Pippen, and Todd Day also have found their way here. The club menu includes Mississippi spaghetti, barbecue ribs, and hot wings. If dancing is your pleasure, this is one spot you'll definitely want to visit during your stay in Memphis.

MIAMI, FLORIDA

For many people, Miami has long represented the ultimate vacation destination, but the past three years have seen a slump in the city's all-important tourist trade. While few signs of Hurricane Andrew remain, undoing the damage caused by widely publicized attacks against tourists in 1992 and 1993 has proved more difficult. Miami has enlisted the entire community to make the city safer for visitors and residents alike. Rental car companies have removed the telltale stickers from all vehicles. Hotels place helpful hints about personal security measures in all rooms. Club managers are quick to point out the security systems they employ or the relative safety of their locations.

During my last visit this past summer, I found Miami as attractive and alluring as ever. Coincidentally, the city was hosting a convention of travel agents whose agenda, I'm told, was to determine if Miami is again a safe tourist destination. Of course, you still must exercise the caution that has become essential for navigating any city today, but my vote is a resounding yes!

Miami's African American community offers enormous opportunity for entrepreneurs, and many African American residents are at the forefront of securing broader participation in the city's economic future. Senator Carrie Meek is the first African American woman to be elected to Florida's Senate. The Reeves family has chronicled African American issues for more than three-quarters of a century in the *Miami Times*, which also plays an important role in the community through its BlackArchives and Resources Foundation. Florida Memorial College has been a major educator of African American youth since 1879. Several new ventures hold enormous promise: the artist formerly known as Prince recently opened a version of his Minneapolis-based Glam Slam Night Club on Miami Beach, and there is a proposed new hotel complex by Atlanta entrepreneur H. G. Russell.

The cultural landscape in Miami has a distinctly Caribbean flavor. One way to get a taste of this is to visit the annual Goombay Festival held each June. Of course, you don't have to wait until then—Miami's warm climate, glorious beaches, and tropical ambience beckon year-round.

MUSIC

MOJAZZ CAFE

Location: 928 71st St. (Miami Beach, Fl.)
Telephone: (305) 865-2636
Clientele: Young/Mature Adult
Format: Jazz/Blues
Calendar: Live Entertainment Nightly (Fall & Winter);
Tues.–Sun. (Spring & Summer)
Cover/Minimum: Yes/Yes (Fri.–Sat.: Music Charge Added
& 1 drink)
Dress: Casual/Classy

Comments: Mo Morgan's Mojazz Cafe has been on the Miami scene less than two years and has already been acclaimed by the *Miami New Times*, an entertainment weekly, as the city's best jazz club. The cafe employs a house-band format featuring local artists, some of whom have national stature. Morgan himself plays sax and handles vocals in front of a straightahead trio with Bill Peeples on drums, Dolph Castellano on piano, and Lew Berryman on bass. Among the local talent the club has featured are keyboard player Doctor Lonnie Smith and horn player Ira Sullivan. The club is both intimate and vibrant. When you walk in, you'll find a solid oak bar with white trim on the left and a dining room on the right. The dining room is L-shaped, a narrow corridor that pauses at the side of the stage and angles left, ending in a small dining area in front of the stage. A string of colorful lights in the front windows and in two corners of the room adds a festive touch to an otherwise laid-back ambience. Mirrors create an illusion of additional space in the room that seats about 100. The only obstructed view is at the far end of the bar. This club has the looks of one with staying power. Mo Morgan, who previously owned the Jazz Mania Society, a loft club in Manhattan, is passionate about the music and about making Mojazz Cafe a staple for jazz in the area. Jazz aficionados will want to put this one at the top of their list when visiting Miami.

89

THE STEPHEN TALKHOUSE

Location: 66 Collins Ave. (Miami Beach, Fl.)
Telephone: (305) 531-7557
Clientele: Young/Mature Adult
Format: Blues/Jazz/Rock/Folk/World Beat
Calendar: Live Entertainment Wed.–Sun.
Cover/Minimum: Yes/No
Dress: Casual/Classy

Comments: The Stephen Talkhouse is Miami's premier music showcase, cited by the *Miami New Times* as the city's "Best Concert venue for 1994." The club is large and airy. A long bar on the left side of the room offers one of the best vantage points from which to see a performance. A narrow passage between the bar and a long bench resembling a church pew allows patrons to file past en route to the rear of the room. Tables are lined up against this bench, in the center of the room, and along a similar, but smaller bench in another corner. Seating in the right corner allows mostly a rear/side profile of the performers on stage. The ambience is eclectic, made so by dim lights and abstract art pieces, many by Marcie Howerkamp, wife of co-owner Peter Howerkamp. The club seats about 250. Here you can catch some of the top artists of not only this country, but the Caribbean and Latin America as well. Blues stars Richie Havens, Etta James, Taj Mahal, and Duke Robillard have been featured. So have Sheila E and E-Train with Latin jazz, Cedric "IM" Brooks with Afro-Caribbean jazz, Bobby Ramirez and Full Power with Brazilian jazz, and Haitian artists Ayabonmbe and Soul Afrika with their unique Creole sound. With such a lineup, The Stephen Talkhouse has to rate among the top choices when considering entertainment options in Miami. A VIP table ticket assures you a seat in the main room near the stage, but they are allocated on a first-come, first-serve basis and guaranteed only until showtime. Reservations are strongly recommended for the larger shows.

90

STUDIO ONE 83: JAZZ ROOM

Location: 2668 NW 183rd St.
Telephone: (305) 621-7295
Clientele: Mature Adult
Format: Jazz/Comedy
Calendar: Live Entertainment Fri.–Tues.
(Jazz: Fri.–Sat.; Comedy: Sun.–Tues.)
Cover/Minimum: Yes/No
Dress: Classy

Comments: The Jazz Room is Miami's longest-running venue for jazz. The club is located in a converted department store in the Colony Square Mall, part of the Studio One 83 entertainment complex. The management has combined the elements of a concert hall, a disco, and a jazz room into one neat package that has been a staple in Miami for more than 15 years. The Jazz Room is the most attractive venue in the complex, with soft lights, crystal chandeliers, and mirrors throughout. A sign above the stage reads "99 JAMS (WEDR)." Ruby Baker and Future are regularly featured. They perform music ranging from contemporary and classical jazz to oldies R & B. The 1960 R & B group War performed a recent promo in conjunction with FM radio station WEDR. The club also offers a wide range of events from Sunday through Thursday. A professional night each Wednesday is designed to promote networking among members of the business community. In addition to the entertainment featured here, the Studio One 83 complex has long been one of the most important facilities in Miami's African American community for hosting community events, from political fundraisers to business symposiums by talk-show host Tony Brown to a concert by gospel singer Shirley Caesar. The Jazz Room seats about 200, while the adjoining banquet facility can hold anywhere from 1,500 to 2,000, depending on the setup. When you're in the city, be sure to stop by the Jazz Room for an entertaining evening, and don't forget to call to find out what's on the calendar for the rest of the Studio One 83 complex.

TOBACCO ROAD

Location: 626 S. Miami Ave.
Telephone: (305) 374-1198
Clientele: Young/Mature Adult
Format: Blues/Jazz
Calendar: Live Entertainment Nightly
Cover/Minimum: Yes/No
Dress: Casual/Classy

Comments: Tobacco Road is one of the oldest blues clubs in the Southeast. Established in 1912, the club also boasts the oldest liquor license in Miami, Number 001. In its early years, it served as a speakeasy. Ask any bartender or waitress, and he or she will gleefully tell you about the secret room upstairs where contraband alcohol was hidden during Prohibition. In 1982, Patrick Gleber and Kevin Rusk purchased the club and converted it to a mecca for blues artists. When you walk through the door, glance to the left, and you'll see photographs of previous artists that depict virtually a history of blues in the United States. Legendary musicians such as Clarence "Gatemouth" Brown, the late Albert Collins, Johnny Copeland, John Lee Hooker, B. B. King, and Charlie Musselwhite have all performed here. One display includes a photo and plaque in memory of longtime employee Willie "Doc Feelgood" Bell. The first-floor bar is a narrow room with booths and a hardwood-topped bar spanning two-thirds of the room, all converging on a small passageway towards the rear and an adjacent stage. Here is where local blues acts most often perform, as do the opening acts for major shows held upstairs. Getting a view of the band from many areas of the room can be a challenge. This area and the patio accommodate about 75 patrons. Upstairs is the Diamond Teeth Mary Cabaret, named in memory of blues and gospel singer Mary Smith McCain. The cabaret has the feel and look of a traditional blues room: red walls, painted black floors, and tables decked with red tablecloths. The room has about 60 seats, all providing a good view of the stage. By day, Tobacco Road is a neighborhood bar. At night, local blues favorite Iko Iko, the house band since 1982, packs them in. After the opening acts perform downstairs, the crowd typically makes a beeline for seats upstairs, so you should plan your strategy accordingly!

92

DINING

BIG JIM'S II BAR-B-QUE

Location: 20712 South Dixie Hwy.
Telephone: (305) 232-9943
Proprietor: The Lewis Family
Menu: Soul Food
Price: Modest
Hours: Tues.–Thurs.: 7:30 A.M.–9:00 P.M.;
Fri.–Sat.: 7:30 A.M.–10:00 P.M.; Sun.: 6:30 A.M.–6:30 P.M.

Comments: Big Jim's II Bar-B-Que is a small roadside cafe located at the southern edge of the city near Homestead, Florida. The menu includes a soulful smorgasbord of ham hocks, chitterlings, barbecue ribs, stew beef, black-eyed peas, and candied yams. Their fried chicken with rice and gravy is the most-requested dish. According to Big Jim's daughter, Lisa Lewis, her father, James Lewis, Sr., opened his first restaurant in 1959. During the late 1980s, Jim Senior and his wife Leila operated two restaurants, Big Jim's I and Big Jim's II. The former closed in 1991. Big Jim's II continued to prosper until Hurricane Andrew mangled the Homestead area in 1992. Jim Lewis, Jr., related that after the storm the restaurant looked as though a freight train has passed through it. The cash register in front had been blown through one wall in back, and iron grates in front of the building had been twisted like pretzels. The family was devastated, but pulled together and carried on. For several months, they operated out of their front yard. Meanwhile, they performed many of the repairs to the building themselves. After much hard work, the restaurant reopened and is steadily recovering its client base. When I asked whether I could come back 50 years from now and find her family operating this business, Lisa Lewis emphatically said, "Yes, it will be Big Lisa's!" To get there from downtown Miami, take the turnpike south, exit at Cutler Ridge, and make a left on South Dixie. It's a few blocks down on the right. Big Jim's is a 15-minute ride from downtown Miami that's well worth the trip.

93

BOCLATIAN RESTAURANT

Location: 18085 NW 27th St.
Telephone: (305) 621-3969
Proprietor: The Williams Family
Dress: Casual
Menu: Soul Food
Price: Moderate
Hours: Tues.–Wed. & Sun.:
8:00 A.M.–8:00 P.M.; Thurs.–Sat.: 8:00 A.M.–9:00 P.M.

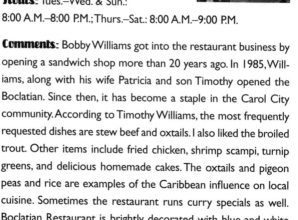

Comments: Bobby Williams got into the restaurant business by opening a sandwich shop more than 20 years ago. In 1985, Williams, along with his wife Patricia and son Timothy opened the Boclatian. Since then, it has become a staple in the Carol City community. According to Timothy Williams, the most frequently requested dishes are stew beef and oxtails. I also liked the broiled trout. Other items include fried chicken, shrimp scampi, turnip greens, and delicious homemade cakes. The oxtails and pigeon peas and rice are examples of the Caribbean influence on local cuisine. Sometimes the restaurant runs curry specials as well. Boclatian Restaurant is brightly decorated with blue-and-white table tops, floral arrangements on each, and potted plants throughout. It is located across the street from the Studio One 83 complex, less than a mile from Miami's Joe Robbie Stadium. As such, it's small wonder why several members of the Dolphins football team and numerous celebrities have stopped by. Good, down-home cooking and Southern ambience are compelling reasons to visit Boclatian Restaurant when you're in the area.

DANCING

AMNESIA

Location: 136 Collins Ave. (South Miami Beach, Fl.)
Telephone: (305) 531-5535
Clientele: Young/Mature Adult
Format: Top 40/International/ World Beat
Calendar: Live Entertainment Varies; Dancing Tues.–Sun.
Cover/Minimum: Yes/No
Dress: Classy

Comments: Amnesia is one of several clubs on South Miami Beach that are part of a circuit traveled by those in the know. The club's unusual concept sets it apart from the rest. This concept, in fact, propels Amnesia into a position as one of the top dance clubs in the Southern United States. Its design is straight out of the era when Rome was an empire. Imagine a small white colosseum rising up from and around a patio with a large stage in front. At the rear of the stage is a sculpture in bas-relief and a waterfall. A dance area, really a covered atrium, on the right side of the patio has the latest in lighting dangling from its white slab cover. Seating is tiered upward, ending in private alcoves, some under cover, throughout. Modular pillow seats in soft tropical colors add to the ambience. A restaurant encased in glass looks down on the patio from the left. The management calls Amnesia "an open sky multi-level disco, covered with canopy." The whole complex accommodates more than 1,000. Amnesia opened in February 1994 and has quickly become one of the "in" spots on Miami Beach. Celebrities such as Wesley Snipes, Sylvester Stalone, and Sharon Stone have dropped by. The club also has hosted record release parties for Latin stars Tito Puente and Jon Secado. The entertainment calendar features everyone from new Latin pop stars Cheito and Marc Anthony to disco-era divas Gloria Gaynor and Thelma Houston. The restaurant serves French cuisine. Reservations are taken, in season, sometimes as much as a week in advance. They are not required for the club. However, sometimes Amnesia will host private parties early in the evening and open the club to the public later, so call ahead. This is one of the must stops in Miami.

STUDIO ONE 83: MIAMI NIGHTS

Location: 2668 NW 183rd St.
Telephone: (305) 621-7295
Clientele: Young/Mature Adult
Format: R & B/House/Reggae
Calendar: Dancing Wed.–Sun.
Cover/Minimum: Yes/No
Dress: Classy

Comments: Miami Nights at Studio One 83 is the city's longest-running, large-format R & B club. A dance floor located in the front of the club dominates the room, with comfortable seating arrayed on both sides. An adjacent room provides a more relaxed setting for patrons who want to retire from the throngs in the dance area. While the complex's banquet area is most often used as a concert showcase, the Miami Nights dance club also has hosted entertainers such as R & B artists Jennifer Holliday, Evelyn "Champagne" King, and En Vogue.

96

MUSIC

MUSICIANS EXCHANGE CAFE

Location: 729 W. Sunrise Blvd.
Telephone: (305) 764-1912
Clientele: Young/Mature Adult
Format: Jazz/Blues/Rock
Calendar: Live Entertainment Varies
Cover/Minimum: Yes/No
Dress: Casual/Classy

Comments: The Musicians Exchange Complex is a large building spanning almost an entire block and housing everything from a recording studio to a rehearsal room to an electronics and repair shop. The Musicians Exchange Cafe is a lounge located on the building's second floor. The stage spans the entire room. Four wooden beams, two near the center and two at the rear of the room, are the only noticeable obstructions to the view of the stage, and these are easily overcome by a slight turn of the head or a nudge of the seat. The tables are solid and compact. A mural at the rear of the room is alive with a stylized keyboard, drum, and sax. The ambience is rounded out by a few scattered, miniature flood lights, oozing pale tints and hues. A number of the greats have played this room. Look at the wall on the right as you enter, and you'll find photos of many of them, jazz standouts Mose Allison, Roy Ayers, Tito Puente, and Stanley Jordan; and blues notables Buddy Guy, Robert Jr. Lockwood, Matt "Guitar" Murphy, and Koko Taylor, to name a few. As of this writing, Musicians Exchange Cafe is contemplating a move to downtown Ft. Lauderdale. Be sure to call ahead when you're in the area to find out what is on their calendar. They're one of the premier blues and jazz showcases in South Florida.

97

RAZOR'S PALACE

Location: 3801 W. Broward Blvd. (Plantation, Fl.)
Telephone: (305) 321-9378
Clientele: Young/Mature Adult
Format: Reggae/R & B/Blues
Calendar: Live Entertainment Thurs.–Fri. & Sun.;
Dancing Weds.–Sun.
Cover/Minimum: Yes/No
Dress: Casual/Classy

Comments: Razor's Palace is an attractive new showcase on the outskirts of Ft. Lauderdale, just north of Miami. The club, located in a building that formerly housed an establishment called Roger's, was founded in 1993 by heavyweight boxer Donovan "Razor" Rudduck. The exterior and interior decor were totally redesigned. Inside, the room is white with charcoal accents, checkered ceramic tiles, wall-mounted mirrors, modular seating, and three U-shaped bars. The room seats 340 with standing room to 400. According to assistant manager Bobby Beans, who managed the Kingston Sheraton in Jamaica for six years, the club's primary focus is oldies and Jamaican and R & B music. A look at some of the artists who have performed there to date bears this out: the Chi-lites, the Drifters, the Manhattans, and Percy Sledge are some of the 1960s standouts who have headlined. I took in their Nostalgia in Gold show this summer, featuring Jamaican legends the Clarendonians, Strangjah Cole, and Larry Marshall, all backed by local reggae favorites, the Mistique Band. Razor's Palace also is fast becoming an important venue for community events such as private parties, banquets, and weddings. This summer, they hosted part of the Sistrunk Historical Festival, an annual event in neighboring Sistrunk that celebrates Native American and African American culture in Florida. They also host the *Caribbean Lifestyles Magazine*'s annual Miss Caribbean Lifestyles beauty contest. The menu features a varied selection of Caribbean, international, and continental cuisine, from jerked pork to curried shrimp and lobster to broiled steaks. Another island favorite, Fish and Bammy, is one of the most-requested dishes: fried kingfish served with a bread made of the cassava and yucca plants—too good to pass up. To get there, take I-95 north to the Broward Exit. Go west, and you'll find Razor's on the right.

NASHVILLE, TENNESSEE

Nashville is considered by some to be the Athens of the South. This is largely due to the numerous and diverse educational institutions throughout the city. Among its "traditionally black colleges," Fisk University, a private Methodist school founded in 1866, is one of Nashville's landmark universities. W. E. B. Du Bois, unarguably one of the most important African American leaders and American civil libertarians of this century, heads a long list of distinguished Fisk graduates. Du Bois's book of essays, *The Souls of Black Folks*, polarized the African American community at the turn of the 20th century. With its publication, Du Bois put himself firmly in opposition to Booker T. Washington. Where Washington espoused conciliation and compromise, Du Bois countered as a voice for activism and change, demanding equality and justice for all Americans regardless of color, creed, or race. Along with two other leading activists of the day, William Trotter and Ida B. Wells, Du Bois helped found the NAACP in 1909.

Meharry Medical College, just around the corner from Fisk, is another landmark institution, founded in 1876. Statistics reported in 1980 indicated that its graduates accounted for more than 40 percent of the nation's practicing African American physicians and dentists. Tennessee State University, established as an agricultural and industrial university in 1909, has long distinguished itself as one of the premier training grounds for African American engineers in the country. Among its best-known graduates are syndicated columnist Carl Rowan, three-time Olympic gold medalist Wilma Rudolph, and actor and talk-show host Oprah Winfrey.

"Music City, U.S.A.," as Nashville is often called, is Tennessee's premier vacation spot. Its country music legacy is widely known, but Nashville has a rich gospel and R & B tradition as well. The Fisk Jubilee Singers are largely responsible for laying the foundations for the worldwide popularity gospel music enjoys today. Their tours of the United States and Europe during the 1870s through the turn of the century gave a world stage to "Negro Spirituals" and a heightened awareness of the condition of African Americans in the South.

Whatever your reason for visiting Nashville, you'll find a rich and culturally diverse landscape, full of attractive entertainment options.

MUSIC

BOARDWALK CAFE

Location: 4114 Nolensville Rd.
Telephone: (615) 832-5104
Clientele: Young/Mature Adult
Format: Blues
Calendar: Live Entertainment Nightly
Cover/Minimum: Yes/No
Dress: Casual

Comments: Boardwalk Cafe is the prototypical blues room. Hardwood floors and tables, knotted pine walls, and posters heralding present and future concerts dominate the room's decor. An old five-gallon coffee pot hangs from the ceiling in the middle of the room, and a vintage World War II aerial bomb hangs in one corner. The room is divided into thirds, with seating on either side of a wide aisle that leads to a hardwood bar in the rear. An adjacent game room holds a pool table and video dart-game machines. An old Texaco gas tank sits at one corner of the stage. The room is softly illuminated, mostly by the concert lights that bring the band into full view. I stopped by during a week in which the club featured successive performances by the hot blues guitar of Jimmy Thackery and the Drivers on one night and the Chicago slide guitar of Little Ed and the Blues Imperials the next. Thackery, former lead guitar for the Nighthawks, packs a mean instrument. He performed to standing ovations as he strolled through the room, playing slide with beer bottles plucked from the tables of appreciative patrons. That's a tough act to follow, but Little Ed gave a lesson in the classic Chicago slide guitar to an equally appreciative audience the following night. Appaloosa recording star Sam Lay and his Blues Band, Blind Pig Record's Chubby Carrier and the Bayou Swamp Band, Rising Son Records' Eddie Burks, and Justice recording artist Tab Benoit represent the club's current booking philosophy. Sundays through Tuesdays honor an age-old Nashville tradition where songwriters come in and showcase their latest work. The menu ranges from continental cuisine to pasta dishes. The club sells burgers by the ton and steamed snow crab by the bushel. The restaurant is open daily for lunch from 11:00 A.M. Owner Rick Moore has given Nashville residents a classic blues room, one that blues aficionados should place at the top of their list when visiting the city.

THE GRAND OF NASHVILLE

Location: 174 3rd Ave. N
Telephone: (615) 256-0770
Clientele: Young/Mature Adult
Format: R & B/Blues
Calendar: Live Entertainment Nightly
Cover/Minimum: Yes/No
Dress: Classy

Comments: The Grand is Nashville's newest entry into the downtown district's entertainment market. *The Tennessean* noted the club's June 1994 grand opening with a front-page feature in its business section. While I went there fully expecting more of a dance venue as the paper had indicated, what I found is best described as a showcase room. The club is located in a stately, two-story 1890s building with a red brick facade. Two larger-than-life 45-rpm discs are displayed in windows at the entrance. The label on one reads "Party 'Round The Clock," and the label on the other reads "Let's Party." The interior of the club sports a sedate green, white, and mauve color scheme, with brass candle holders as table accents, wall-panel mirrors, and potted plants all around. A mauve, U-shaped reception booth greets entering patrons. A wall at the rear of the stage is alive with different hues of red and brown bricks. According to co-owner Jazy Stroman, former backup singer with the 1960s R & B group, the Flamingos, the club's mission is to provide a showcase for local R & B acts as well as regional and national R & B, blues, and jazz performers. R & B star Dorothy Moore headlined at the club's grand opening.

101

MÈRE BULLES

Location: 152 2nd Ave. N
Telephone: (615) 256-1946
Clientele: Young/Mature Adult
Format: Jazz/R & B
Calendar: Live Entertainment Thurs.–Sat.
Cover/Minimum: Yes/No
Dress: Casual

Comments: Founded in 1988, Mère Bulles consistently has provided Nashville's most sophisticated jazz, dancing, and dining experience. The club and restaurant are located in the old Maxwell House Coffee warehouse, dating back to the late 1800s. Situated on the ground floor, Mère Bulles is a rectangular complex that spans almost a city block. The club and restaurant are divided into four distinct segments beginning with a cocktail bar on the right and mahogany booths on the left. Tables laminated in bronze and gold are placed next to the booths, forming a line that ends at a raised, hardwood stage on the right side of the room and at another mahogany bar on the left. A partition at the end of this bar, inset with glass and etched in white, separates the lounge area from an elegant dining room in the rear. The first dining area reveals an archway that leads to three separate dining alcoves, each with large picture windows that provide a romantic view of the Cumberland River. The decor is complemented by impressionistic and abstract oils, the works of local artists Frank Ferra and Arthur Kirby respectively. Light green tablecloths, fresh-cut flowers, a wine cellar, and a fireplace round out the decor in each dining room. James Otey and the Imperials, the group that once featured Little Anthony, are a regular feature. So are Tabitha and the New Day Band, the San Rafael Band, and Friction. The music ranges from straightahead and contemporary to Brazilian jazz. Pan-sauteed sea bass, grilled yellowfin tuna, and Cajun-style rock shrimp are some of the delicacies available in the dining room; smoked salmon, dim sum (pork dumplings served with rice-wine sauce), and club sandwiches are available in the lounge. For an evening of jazz and fine dining, put this one at the top of your list when visiting Music City.

102

THE SUTLER

Location: 2608 Franklin Rd.
Telephone: (615) 297-9195
Clientele: Young/Mature Adult
Format: Blues/Rock/Alternative
Calendar: Live Entertainment Varies
Cover/Minimum: Yes/No
Dress: Casual

Comments: The Sutler is one of the most unusual blues rooms in the Southeast. Like most, it's cozy and comfortable, but its ambience differs somewhat due to the eclectic nature of the decor. Nineteenth-century nude photographs occupy prominent positions along the walls, vying for attention with Civil War memorabilia and music posters. A large, colorful totem pole with a thunderbird at its apex sits in one corner of the room. A hand-carved back bar that, according to a narrative on the menu, dates to 1875, stands behind the sit-down bar. The main room wraps around the stage to provide unobstructed views for all of the cocktail tables. The line-up of entertainment for the Sutler includes local, regional, and, on occasion, touring acts. Steve Ferguson and the Midwest Creole Ensemble, Jimmy Hall and the Prisoners of Love, Hal Newman and the Mystics of Time, Johnny Neel and the Last Word, the Nighthawks, and the Amy Watkins Blues Band are some of the acts that have been featured. The Sutler has been on the Nashville scene since the mid-1970s and continues to be one of the city's most important blues venues. For information on the Sutler and other blues happenings, call the Music City Blues Society's free, 24-hour hotline at (615) 292-5222.

3RD & LINSLEY BAR AND GRILL

Location: 818 3rd Ave. S
Telephone: (615) 259-9891/766-3009
Clientele: Young/Mature Adult
Format: Blues/Folk/R & B
Calendar: Live Entertainment Mon.–Sat.
Cover/Minimum: Yes/No
Dress: Casual

Comments: The 3rd & Linsley Bar and Grill is a cozy, L-shaped room with green and lavender accents. High ceilings and large steam pipes course throughout. A kitchen and a small dining room are located to the right of the bar; each table in the main dining room offers a good view of the band. However, bar seats may be somewhat obstructed by two small support beams. Stylized paintings of musicians by artist Frank Ferra are displayed all around the room. A tiny loft upstairs is one of the favorite vantage points for enjoying live performances. The place seats 190 comfortably. Founded in 1992, 3rd & Lindsley has quickly become one of Nashville's most important blues venues. The club does a promo with Tom Kats Productions and WRLT FM 100. Each Thursday night during the summer, the latter features touring acts in a popular happening at Riverfront Park called Dancing in the District. When the party concludes downtown, it moves inside, culminating at 3rd & Lindsley. The club also serves as the back-up venue during inclement weather. The 3rd & Lindsley Bar and Grill initially began as a spot for local bands, but has, of late, expanded to include regional and national acts. Celinda Pink and the Cellar Dwellers are a local favorite. Guitarist Terry Garland, a transplant from Richmond, Virginia, can also be heard here when not on tour. Mary-Ann Brandon, Jimmy Hall and the Prisoners of Love, the Reverend Billy C. Wirtz, and the Steve Schuffert Band have also performed. The grill stakes a claim to the best cheeseburger in town. Get there by 8:30 P.M. to get your choice of seating. The room quickly begins to fill by 9:00 P.M.

DINING

ED'S FISH

Location: 1801 Dr. D. B. Todd, Jr., Blvd.
Telephone: (615) 255-4362
Proprietor: Anthony
& Pam Drumwright
Dress: Casual/Classy
Menu: Fish
Price: Very Modest
Hours: Mon.–Wed.: 11:00 A.M.–10:00 P.M.;
Thurs.: 11:00 A.M.–12:00 A.M.; Fri.–Sat.: 11:00 A.M.–4:00 A.M.
(Drive-through to 11:00 P.M. Thurs.–Sat.)

Comments: Ed's Fish has long been a favorite of students at Fisk University, Meharry Medical College, and Tennessee State University. When alumni return for class reunions or homecoming festivities, this is one of their first stops in retracing the steps of their college days. The restaurant is a tiny blue-and-white cottage trimmed in brownstone. Its outline is traced in red, green, and white neon lights at night. Blue-and-white tiles cover the walls and countertop. The kitchen, visible from the counter, is always bustling with activity. The service is take-out or drive-through. Anthony and Pam Drumwright have owned the restaurant for the past few years. It was founded by their cousin, Edward A. Moins, Jr. Deep-fried whiting served between two slices of white bread remains the staple of the restaurant. Long-time patrons come in and order theirs either "with" or "without"—pickles, onions, and mustard, that is. The fish plate with cole slaw, spaghetti, onions, pickles, and hot peppers is also popular. Their fresh, homemade sweet-potato and chess pies evoke fond memories, too. The chess pie is by far the more popular, made with cornmeal, but firm and sweet. Enjoy a culinary experience that students of Fisk, Meharry, and T.S.U. have known for almost 20 years.

MODERN ERA RESTAURANT

Location: 1114 Charlotte Ave.

Telephone: (615) 256-5363

Proprietor: Johnny Jones

Dress: Casual

Menu: Soul Food

Price: Very Modest

Hours: Mon.–Thurs.: 12:00 P.M.–10:00 P.M.; Fri.: 12:00 P.M.–12:00 A.M.; Sat.: 2:00 P.M.–12:00 A.M.; Sun.: 1:00 P.M.–7:00 P.M.

Comments: The Modern Era Restaurant, aka New Era Restaurant, is a tiny soul-food take-out. Bare concrete walls and a serving line are the dominant features of this roadside eatery. Steaming-hot serving trays are filled with traditional soul-food fare such as chitterlings, ham hocks, smothered pork chops, fried chicken, candied yams, and turnip greens. In a small corner behind the serving counter, the restaurant's owner, Johnny Jones, can often be found cleaning the chitterlings or washing the greens. This is a place that frequently is mentioned during conversations with local residents about the city's best soul-food offerings. The New Era has a bulletin board that is best described as a testament to the blues, with its autographed photographs of Johnny Copeland, B. B. King, and Johnny "Guitar" Watson. There also are photos of the restaurant's owner playing slide guitar with some of these legends. An old newspaper article, perhaps from *The Tennessean*, at the center of the board offers an explanation. Johnny Jones toured with many of these artists during the early 1960s. Swapping the trials of the road for more stability, he convinced the owners of the Modern Era Lounge next door to let him turn their convenience store into a soul-food eatery during the early 1980s. Someday, Jones claims, he's going to get back in the studio. This restaurant is full of surprises. Adjoining it is the second-largest R & B party in Nashville, the Modern Era Lounge. Many of the acts on the historic "Chittlin' Circuit" played this room. The club dates back to the mid-1950s and has been at its current location since the mid-1960s. These days, it's mostly a neighborhood R & B club, albeit one that is filled to its capacity of more than 400 on most weekends.

SWETT'S RESTAURANT

Location: 2725 Clifton Ave.
Telephone: (615) 329-4418
Proprietor: The Swett Family
Dress: Casual/Classy
Menu: Soul Food/Southern
Price: Very Modest
Hours: Daily: 11:00 A.M.–9:00 P.M.

Comments: Swett's is Nashville's largest and most popular soul-food restaurant. The restaurant sits at the far end of the parking lot on the corner of Clifton and 28th. The main dining room, on the right as you enter, is swathed in red brick and soft lavender. The outer portion of the dining room is a cozy patio encased in glass. The opposite side of the building consists of a dining room with similar decor; this is most often used when the main room overflows or for private parties. The entire facility seats almost 200. A long serving line, partially concealed from view in the main dining room, holds trays of piping-hot dishes such as meatloaf, fried chicken, smothered pork chops, fried catfish, candied yams, steamed cabbage, turnip greens, and hoe cakes. Their beef tips, diced beef in a mushroom gravy, are the most requested entree. Susie and Walter Swett founded the restaurant in 1954. Starting out in a little white building on the corner of their current location, it was a modest affair that sold beer and sandwiches. Shortly after opening, Susie Swett decided to prepare a full meal that included chitterlings, turnips, green beans, and yams just to see how the items would sell. It was an instant success. By the early 1960s, the Swetts weren't selling much beer, but they were selling a lot of soul food. In 1972, they remodeled the restaurant and featured the current cafeteria style. Walter Swett retired in 1979, selling the restaurant to sons David Senior and Morris. In 1988, they built a larger, more modern restaurant that was destroyed by fire within 30 days of its completion. They held the grand reopening of the current facility in April 1989. A third generation of Swetts, David Junior and Patrick, work at the restaurant. Another son, Alberto, and daughter Nikki help out during the summer. This is a family affair celebrating its 40th anniversary in the business. Be sure to stop in and enjoy some down-home cooking when you're visiting Nashville.

DANCING

CLUB MÈRE BULLES

Location: 152 2nd Ave. N
Telephone: (615) 256-CLUB
Clientele: Young/Mature Adult
Format: Top 40/R & B
Calendar: Live
Entertainment Wed.–Sun.
Cover/Minimum: Yes/No
Dress: Classy

Comments: Club Mère Bulles is located in the basement of the building housing the restaurant and bar, Mère Bulles. It is similar in decor to the lounge upstairs, with two solid oak bars at each end and a large hardwood dance floor and stage in the center of the room. Traffic Jam, the Jimmy Church Band, the MAXX, and Familiar Faces are among the bands who regularly are featured. Dress for success and stop by for an evening of top-flight entertainment and dancing after a meal upstairs.

MALIBU BEACH CLUB

Location: 115 Cumberland Bend
Telephone: (615) 251-8003
Clientele: Young/Mature Adult
Format: R & B/Jazz/Blues/Top 40
Calendar: Live Entertainment Fri.–Sat.; Dancing Wed.–Sun.
Cover/Minimum: Yes/No
Dress: Classy

Comments: Malibu Beach Club is among the top five R & B clubs in the southeastern United States. The decor is dolphin blue and fuchsia both inside and out. The building sits at the edge of a picturesque pond on a 250-acre complex called the Metro Center. A striking facility on stilts, the Malibu Beach Club is illuminated at night to achieve an iridescent glow. The interior features long, comfortable lounge sofas at the entrance, tall cocktail tables and stools of fuchsia and dolphin blue. The interior walls are crafted to replicate the facades of village cottages. A deejay booth is housed in one such structure, a mezzanine overlooking the dance floor. Potted plants throughout and an aquarium under the deejay booth round out the decor. The entire facility includes a sports bar seating about 30, the main entertainment room accommodating 650, and a cabana seating 120. While Malibu Beach primarily is a dance club, the cabana room features live entertainment on Friday and Saturday nights. Local R & B phenomenon Jane Powell is a regular feature. The club also hosts touring acts each month. Jazz standouts Stanley Jordan, Micki Howard, and the Jazz Crusaders have already played the room since its grand opening in March 1994. Former professional basketball stars Michael Jordan and Maurice Lucas are among the celebrities who have dropped in. Local entrepreneur Guy Rogers has been in the club business around Nashville for more than a quarter of a century. This is certainly his most stunning achievement to date. According to managing partner Lance Lester, this venture was one that Nashville needed. In addition to its popularity as a dance and entertainment showcase, the club is fast becoming one of Nashville's most-requested venues for private parties, wedding receptions, and civic promotions. This one has few rivals in the Southeast.

109

NEW ORLEANS, LOUISIANA

New Orleans is the spirit of the South. Although the language of the city is obviously English, the flavor is French and Spanish. New Orleans' essence is appropriately manifested in its rich jazz heritage. While blues and ragtime were being forged in the Mississippi Delta and Missouri Valley in the late 1800s, African Americans in the Crescent City were absorbing this new music and adding their own distinctive flair. This merger of France, Spain and Africa also reveals itself in the city's Creole and Cajun cuisines.

According to many historians, New Orleans is the city that gave birth to America's unique musical art form, jazz, in the late 1890s when coronetist Buddy Bolden emerged as the city's leading practitioner of the new blues and ragtime movement. Brass bands had begun to spring up all over the city. By the turn of the century, these bands, most notably Buddy Bolden's, had developed a style of music where the beat was syncopated and the musicians free to improvise collectively. Native son Louis "Satchmo" Armstrong was pivotal in taking this art form to lofty heights as the United States' musical ambassador from the early 1930s to 1971, the last year of his life.

The list of famous New Orleans musicians is long and distinguished. In jazz, there was Jelly Roll Morton, Joe "King" Oliver and Edward "Kid" Ory. In blues, there is Antoine "Fats" Domino and departed stars such as Lizzie Douglas aka Memphis Minnie, long-time resident Professor Longhair, and nearby Lafayette Louisiana's Clifton Chenier, to name a few. The city's musical roots run deep. Trombonist Lucien Barbarin traces his lineage back to five generations of musical Barbarins such as his great-uncle Isidore Barbarin, a leader of one of the city's early brass bands. Ellis Marsalis leads a musical family whose influence is felt worldwide. Aaron Neville and his talented siblings also share this mantle of musical creativity. Clarinetist Alvin Batiste is also an important artist in the city's constellation of stars.

While thousands flock to the world-famous annual Mardi Gras celebration, the Crescent City offers many other attractions that make a visit there memorable any time of the year.

MUSIC

CAFE BRASIL

Location: 2100 Chartres St.
Telephone: (504) 947-9386
Clientele: Young/Mature Adult
Format: Jazz/Reggae
Calendar: Live Entertainment Nightly
Cover/Minimum: Yes/No
Dress: Casual/Classy

Comments: Cafe Brasil is a large, festive club located at the edge of the French Quarter. The room is dominated by white walls illuminated by soft neon lights. The panorama of the street outside, viewed through the glass windows and doors that ring the club, gives it an even lighter feel. Except for a black-and-green bar and a few scattered bar stools, the club is one giant dance floor. Outside, on most weekends the scene is reminiscent of a block party. Many patrons alternate between this club and Cafe Istanbul, just across the street. Both offer reggae, salsa, and calypso, although Cafe Brasil's primary emphasis is Latin jazz. The crowd tends toward the younger set; however, you'll often find an older group who keeps pace with the party.

111

HOUSE OF BLUES

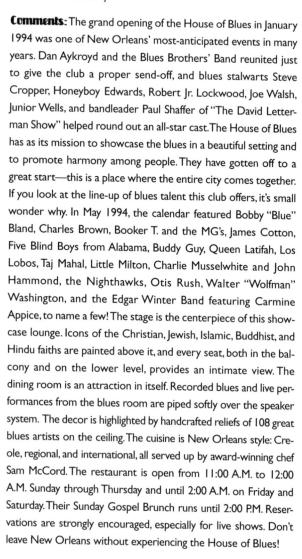

Location: 225 Decatur St.
Telephone: (504) 529-2624
Clientele: Young/Mature Adult
Format: Blues/Jazz/R & B/Zydeco
Calendar: Live Entertainment Nightly
Cover/Minimum: Yes/No
Dress: Casual/Classy

Comments: The grand opening of the House of Blues in January 1994 was one of New Orleans' most-anticipated events in many years. Dan Aykroyd and the Blues Brothers' Band reunited just to give the club a proper send-off, and blues stalwarts Steve Cropper, Honeyboy Edwards, Robert Jr. Lockwood, Joe Walsh, Junior Wells, and bandleader Paul Shaffer of "The David Letterman Show" helped round out an all-star cast. The House of Blues has as its mission to showcase the blues in a beautiful setting and to promote harmony among people. They have gotten off to a great start—this is a place where the entire city comes together. If you look at the line-up of blues talent this club offers, it's small wonder why. In May 1994, the calendar featured Bobby "Blue" Bland, Charles Brown, Booker T. and the MG's, James Cotton, Five Blind Boys from Alabama, Buddy Guy, Queen Latifah, Los Lobos, Taj Mahal, Little Milton, Charlie Musselwhite and John Hammond, the Nighthawks, Otis Rush, Walter "Wolfman" Washington, and the Edgar Winter Band featuring Carmine Appice, to name a few! The stage is the centerpiece of this showcase lounge. Icons of the Christian, Jewish, Islamic, Buddhist, and Hindu faiths are painted above it, and every seat, both in the balcony and on the lower level, provides an intimate view. The dining room is an attraction in itself. Recorded blues and live performances from the blues room are piped softly over the speaker system. The decor is highlighted by handcrafted reliefs of 108 great blues artists on the ceiling. The cuisine is New Orleans style: Creole, regional, and international, all served up by award-winning chef Sam McCord. The restaurant is open from 11:00 A.M. to 12:00 A.M. Sunday through Thursday and until 2:00 A.M. on Friday and Saturday. Their Sunday Gospel Brunch runs until 2:00 P.M. Reservations are strongly encouraged, especially for live shows. Don't leave New Orleans without experiencing the House of Blues!

MAISON BOURBON

Location: 641 Bourbon St.
Telephone: (504) 522-8818
Clientele: Young/Mature Adult
Format: Jazz
Calendar: Live Entertainment Nightly
Cover/Minimum: No/Yes (1 Drink)
Dress: Casual/Classy

Comments: Maison Bourbon is a cozy club like many that have appeared on Bourbon Street. The music can run from touristy to scintillating. The hottest moments occur when artists such as Wallace Davenport command the stage. The venerable Thomas Jefferson also puts in an occasional appearance. A poster on the wall puts it succinctly: "Maison Bourbon recommends Thomas Jefferson." The show runs every 45 minutes beginning at 2:15 P.M. and continues through midnight.

113

MARGARITAVILLE

Location: 1104 Decatur St.

Telephone: (504) 592-2565

Clientele: Young/Mature Adult

Format: R & B/Cajun/Zydeco

Calendar: Live Entertainment Tues.–Sat.

Cover: Yes/No

Dress: Casual/Classy

Comments: Margaritaville, since its founding in 1993, has emerged as one of the city's most important venues for showcasing the unique rhythms and blues of New Orleans musicians. The building has not always been so—its dubious past includes serving as a slave auction house in the early 1800s and later, as a brothel for children. In more recent times, it housed the Storyville nightclub, also a showcase for New Orleans music, but still rather stark and bare. Singer and author Jimmy Buffet and Sunshine Smith took over the property in 1993 and redeemed it as Margaritaville. The building is now awash in a sea of tropical colors and hues. Replicas of parrots and fish are either suspended from the ceiling or nestled along the walls. As you enter, a grand piano sits on the left, and a small bar is situated at the rear. A low wall divides this section from the main dining room filled with tables spaced comfortably apart and adorned with floral tablecloths wrapped snugly in clear vinyl. The dining room seats 250 easily, while the bar side accommodates another 150 standing. Jimmy Buffet plays Margaritaville every six to eight weeks. Local songstress Charmane Neville is a monthly feature. So are one of the area's most popular Cajun groups, Evangeline. Zydeco star Zachary Richard performs at the club three times a year. Local comedians are finding the club an important avenue for their talents. Margaritaville also donates one night monthly as a benefit for the homeless, an event that has attracted such star performers as the Neville Brothers. The restaurant is well known for a menu that is an eclectic blend of New Orleans and the Islands: from red beans and rice, its "Cheeseburger in Paradise: We serve it like the song says," and "blackened hot dog: AKA B.H.D., a Cajun style" to Bahamian-style conch chowder, hand-cut fries, and key lime pie. This is a fun place, whether you are coming for a meal or an outstanding show.

MAXWELL'S TOULOUSE CABARET

Location: 615 Toulouse St.
Telephone: (504) 523-4207
Clientele: Young/Mature Adult
Format: Jazz
Calendar: Live Entertainment Nightly
Cover/Minimum: Yes
(includes 1 drink)/No
Dress: Casual/Classy

Comments: Maxwell's Toulouse Cabaret captures the attention the moment you walk in. The little bar in front is bursting with color. The multicolored "Second Line" umbrellas that are very much a feature of Mardi Gras parades and jazz funerals hang from the rafters. Posters depicting some of the city's jazz legends vie for your attention. A musical "family tree" shows the origins of African American music and its influence on American music in general. The grand cabaret is as subtle as the entrance is not. Cocktail tables are comfortably arrayed on four levels that slope down towards the stage. That's where your attention is riveted, to the music, traditional New Orleans jazz. On any given evening, you can catch performances by the likes of Harry Connick, Sr., Judy Garland, the Sounds of New Orleans featuring Rene Netto, or the New Orleans Kings of Rhythm. During a performance by the latter, patrons shouted out in exultation as the band played "How Come You Do Me Like You Do Do Do" and "Down By the Riverside." They even took a request for "The Yellow Eyes of Texas" and jazzed it up to the delight of a group from Austin. Every set normally ends in New Orleans' traditional dance, the "Second Line." There's not a bad seat in the house. The Maxwell family is a fixture in New Orleans entertainment. Pianist Jimmy Maxwell and His Orchestra play the most exclusive venues in the city, including the family's own cabaret. By day, Maxwell runs the New Orleans Entertainment Agency, managing the city's top entertainers. Maxwell's sister and brother, Peggy and John, run the day-to-day operations of the cabaret. Their mom Joy makes all the umbrellas by hand. Their father, drummer Ed Maxwell, occasionally sits in with Maxwell's orchestra. This is a fun place to bring friends and family. Sets run at 8:00, 9:00, and 10:00 P.M. nightly. Reservations are encouraged.

115

OLD ABSINTHE HOUSE BAR

Location: 400 Bourbon St.
Telephone: (504) 525-8108
Clientele: Young/Mature Adult
Format: Blues
Calendar: Live Entertainment Nightly
Cover/Minimum: No/Yes (1 drink)
Dress: Casual/Classy

Comments: The Old Absinthe House Bar has changed very little since its foundation was laid in 1806. Legend has it that the privateer Jean LaFitte considered this his personal watering hole when he plied the waters of the Caribbean and the Louisiana Gulf Coast. According to club manager Larry Geer, LaFitte would bring his cargo into the city and advertise his wares on a chalkboard at the bar. When absinthe was brought into New Orleans by the French during the 1830s, a number of establishments that sold the drug sprang up across the city, all calling themselves Absinthe House. There is yet another Absinthe House, containing one of the French Quarter's most famous restaurants and bearing a National Historic Register Marker, one block up from this location. From the late 1950s through the early 1980s, the Old Absinthe House Bar has featured everything from popular plays to reggae. In 1983, the bar began featuring Bryan Lee and the Jump Street Five. Their popularity has grown to the point that they are virtually synonymous with Old Absinthe House. Playing a range of blues from country to jumpin' to urban, they provide a compelling reason to drop in and sample the action. The club is a narrow little room with tables scattered throughout. Dollar bills line the walls, dating back to World War II, when the young men of the neighborhood would post dollar bills as talismans to ensure their safe return from the war. The All Purpose Blues band alternates a couple of nights each week. The club has been featured in *Rolling Stone* magazine, in all of the city's local publications and guides, as well as in numerous European travel guides. Getting there early assures a seat nearest the band.

NEW SHOWCASE LOUNGE

Location: 1951 N. Broad St.
Telephone: (504) 945-5612
Clientele: Young/Mature Adult
Format: Jazz/Blues/R & B
Calendar: Live Entertainment
Wed. & Sat.
Dress: Casual/Classy

Comments: This is the quintessential neighborhood bar, New Orleans style, but rather on the tough side. It's a local joint whose popularity has exploded well beyond its own environs. New Showcase Lounge throbs and flows. Outside the quaint and homey building, you'll find cars parked everywhere—along the streets, on the meridians—a sure sign that this is a happening. Inside, there's a piano-shaped bar with a white-brick facade and bar stools with red vinyl cushions. Red lights rhythmically trace the bar's outline overhead. Small cocktail tables bedecked in red cram the main room opposite the bar. A sign in the corner reads "all you can eat buffet: $6.00." The Snap Bean Band led by drummer Walter Payton and featuring the diminutive dynamo Sharon Martin packs them in every Sunday night. Playing a range of music from straightahead to Oleta Adams to traditional blues, they've found an appreciative audience in a house that takes you back to the Crescent City as it was during the 1960s. Patrons spontaneously sing along, dance in the aisles, or laugh approvingly when vocalist Martin coaxes a local regular called "O. C." on stage where he'll do the James Brown slide as the band rocks to Brown's "I Feel Good."

PALM COURT JAZZ CAFE

Location: 1204 Decatur St.
Telephone: (504) 525-0200
Clientele: Young/Mature Adult
Format: Jazz
Calendar: Live Entertainment Wed.–Sun.
Cover/Minimum: Yes/No
Dress: Classy

Comments: Palm Court Jazz Cafe is the most popular jazz supper club in the French Quarter that exclusively showcases local jazz talent. Founder Nina Buck has worked as a booking agent for jazz tours throughout Europe. Her husband, George Buck, Jr., is one of the United States' key figures in the preservation of jazz, having founded both the Jazzology and GHB record labels. Nina Buck set out to give this club, originally a warehouse, an "old New Orleans" feel when she designed it in 1989. The renovations took almost a year. Danny Barker was the club's first headliner. Palm Court Jazz Cafe is attractively decorated in wood paneling and bricks against a white background. Several mannequins attired in 1930s fashions are poised throughout the dining room. A display case holds memorabilia associated with the late trumpet virtuoso Bunk Johnson. Lining the walls is a museum-quality collection of photographs of other New Orleans legends such as drummer Milford Dolliole and trombonist Louis Nelson. A widely traveled and recorded artist, Nelson found Palm Court to his liking and led his own band, the Palm Court Jazz Cafe Band, there for almost a year before he passed away. Dixieland clarinetist and Jazzology recording star Pud Brown plays Palm Court Jazz Cafe Friday through Saturday with a variety of talented New Orleans musicians. Trumpeter Greg Stafford leads the late Danny Barker's band, the Jazz Hounds, on Wednesdays, while Percy Humphrey and the Crescent City Joymakers perform each Thursday. Palm Court Jazz Cafe is the best place in the city to hear New Orleans favorites on a consistent basis. Additionally, the Creole menu features such entrees as their delicious shrimp Creole, a delicately spiced dish of plump Gulf shrimp served on a bed of white rice. Every seat in the dining room offers a good view of the stage. Reservations are strongly encouraged and are the best way to ensure seating near the band.

PATOUT'S & JELLY ROLL'S

Location: 501 Bourbon St.
Telephone: (504) 524-4054/568-0501
Clientele: Young/Mature Adult
Format: Jazz/R & B
Calendar: Live Entertainment Thurs.–Mon.
Cover/Minimum: Patout's: No/No;
Jelly Roll's: Yes (includes dinner)/na
Dress: Casual/Classy

Comments: Patout's is one of the French Quarter's newest jazz supper clubs. Chef Gigi Patout serves up traditional jazz and Cajun cuisine downstairs amid a cozy environment that is upscale but laid-back. The dining room is an airy cafe with a Mediterranean feel: white tablecloths, potted plants, and shutters opening out onto Bourbon Street. Upstairs, Jelly Roll's has the atmosphere of a typical hotel banquet room. Somewhat bare, it's brought alive by touring acts such as New Orleans jazz star Al Hirt. The Patout family emigrated to the United States from France in 1825. Finding the soil more suited to sugarcane than to the grapes they originally had intended to grow, they prospered. According to Chef Patout, theirs is the oldest family-owned and operated sugar mill in the United States. Patout's grandfather founded the first hotel in New Iberia. His father came home from Europe and World War II bent on leaving the hotel business and going into the restaurant trade. After graduating from culinary school at Mississippi State, he returned to New Iberia and established a culinary tradition there that has been passed on to Gigi and her brother, Alex Gerald. In 1991, they founded Patout's and teamed with Phillip and Bobbi Gattuso, who have owned clubs on New Orleans' West Bank for a number of years, to open Jelly Roll's. The specialties of the house are crawfish enchiladas, crawfish cakes, bread pudding, and a spinach and artichoke dish. Patout's is another excellent choice for experiencing the diversity of the city's historic French Quarter. Whether it's for a meal and local jazz at Patout's, or for a national touring act such as Charmane Neville or Al Hirt at Jelly Roll's, stop by. Reservations are encouraged.

119

PRESERVATION HALL

Location: 726 St. Peter St.
Telephone: (504) 522-2841
Clientele: Mature Adult
Format: Jazz
Calendar: Live Entertainment Nightly
Cover/Minimum: Yes/na
Dress: Casual

Comments: Founded in 1961, Preservation Hall is synonymous with the grand tradition of New Orleans jazz. You'll have to stand in line at the door, but the short wait is well worthwhile. One of the oldest-running jazz clubs in the French Quarter, the building radiates history and a sense of timelessness. When you enter, you'll find a small room with limited seating. Many patrons sit on cushions placed just in front of the band. Others sit on several wooden benches in the middle of the room, while latecomers jockey for a view of the band from the rear. What you get for a mere $3.00 cover is 30 to 45 minutes with the Preservation Hall Band, glorious musicians who will have you coming back for more traditional New Orleans jazz night after night. These short sets provide revealing glimpses into the magic of the music to which the city gave birth. Preservation Hall is a must during your stay in New Orleans.

SNUG HARBOR

Location: 626 Frenchmen St.
Telephone: (504) 949-0696
Clientele: Young/Mature Adult
Format: Jazz
Calendar: Live Entertainment Nightly
Cover/Minimum: Yes/No
Dress: Classy

Comments: Snug Harbor is a beautiful jazz club located at the edge of the French Quarter. The atmosphere is just as the name implies: its several rooms are alcoves giving the illusion of a safe refuge from even the most violent storm. The dining room serves moderately priced seafood and continental cuisine. The jazz room is a two-story gem located at the rear of the building. More than a club, it can be aptly described as a listening room. This is very evident when you catch a show by the soft-spoken pianist Ellis Marsalis. On one visit, I heard him accompanied by his son Jason on drums and David Polthus on bass. Two Marsalis students, saxophonist Victor Goines and vocalist Roderick Harper, were invited onstage to showcase their talents as well. The audience was as quiet as any I've heard, except during moments when the music became so good, the interplay between piano, bass, and drums so intricate, that affirmation was due in the form of spontaneous applause. Snug Harbor is a key venue for ensuring the continuation of New Orleans' rich jazz heritage. The Ellis Marsalis Trio is featured most Saturday evenings. Charmane Neville, the Nicholas Payton Group, and Steve Masakowski and Company are also regularly featured. A new group of young stars such as prodigy pianist Nicholas Payton, son of bassist Walter Payton, and Germane Bazzle, whom Snug Harbor owner George Brumet considers the grand dame of New Orleans jazz, are poised to continue a tradition started by Wynton Marsalis and Harry Connick, Jr., both of whom cut their teeth here. Snug Harbor serves dinner from 5:00 P.M. to around midnight. Shows generally consist of two sets, scheduled nightly at 9:00 and 11:00 P.M. Reservations are encouraged for each show. A typical Marsalis performance, for example, will often sell out before 6:00 P.M. Patrons usually begin queuing up about 45 minutes before each show, so get there early.

TIPITINA'S

Location: 501 Napoleon Ave.
Telephone: (504) 895-8477
Clientele: Young/Mature Adult
Format: Blues/Reggae/R & B/Zydeco/Rock & Roll
Calendar: Live Entertainment Nightly
Cover/Minimum: Yes/No
Dress: Casual/Classy

Comments: Since its inception nearly two decades ago, the legendary Tipitina's has been an important venue for New Orleans musicians. In fact, the late Professor Longhair was one of the club's founders. At the entrance of Tipitina's, a bronze bust of Henry Roeland Byrd, which was Professor Longhair's given name, sits poised atop fine granite. Scores of posters from concerts past line the walls near the ceiling: Buckwheat Zydeco, War, Marva Wright, Bobby "Blue" Bland, Bonnie Raitt, and Stanley Jordan, to name a few. The Neville Brothers are a popular monthly attraction. Tipitina's is foremost a dance club. Aside from the stage and two large bars on either side of the first floor, the whole room, devoid of chairs and tables, is a sea of dancers. For some shows, such as a recent performance by native blues star Marva Wright, chairs are set up concert style, ten or so rows deep, nine or so across. Even though the audience gave Wright rapt attention as she belted out her classic blues standards, she entreated her audience to dance because, after all, "This is Tipitina's!" When your appetite grows while dancing the night away or grooving to the beat of blues, jazz, or zydeco rhythms, try the menu featuring New Orleans staples such as jambalaya, gumbo, shrimp and oyster po-boys, or for the adventurous, deep-fried alligator, a dish that many compare to veal or chicken. This is a relatively new club when compared to others you would describe as "institutions." However, that's what Tipitina's is. Tipitina's is a definite must when you're visiting New Orleans.

DINING

DOOKY CHASE

Location: 2301 Orleans St.
Telephone: (504) 821-0600
Proprietor: The Chase Family
Dress: Casual/Classy
Menu: Creole
Price: Modest
Hours: Daily: 11:30 A.M.–12:00 A.M.

Comments: When Edgar "Dooky" Chase, Sr., founded this restaurant in 1941, he gave the city a treasure. Dooky Junior now heads the enterprise, while the family matriarch, Leah, is the restaurant's head chef and spokesperson. Their Creole and seafood fare is legend throughout Louisiana and much of the country. Patrons of Dooky Chase range from tourists who drop by because they have heard of the restaurant or read Leah Chase's cookbook to old faithfuls who have been customers for decades. The delicious lunch buffet includes fried chicken, breaded veal, smoked sausage, gumbo, red beans and rice, string beans, and French bread. Highlights from the dinner menu are "breast of chicken a la Dooky," stuffed lobster or shrimp, shrimp Creole, crawfish etoufee, and court bouillon. For dessert, try the mouthwatering lemon meringue pie or the praline pudding. Leah Chase is perhaps one of the best-known African American chefs in the United States. She has done cooking segments on local and regional television shows, been featured on the popular "Regis and Kathy Lee Live" talk show, and has inspired numerous articles in newspapers and magazines throughout the country. In the course of her career, she has entertained and developed friendships with many of the legends of jazz, R & B, and popular music. Harry Belafonte, Nat King Cole, Billy Eckstine, Duke Ellington, and Sarah Vaughan are names and faces that she recalls easily, guests of the restaurant when Dooky Chase was the most exclusive place in town for African Americans. Dooky's remains one of my favorites. You'd have to search high and wide to find a more elegant, down-home dining establishment, especially one with a hostess like Leah Chase. New Orleans cannot be fully appreciated unless you include Dooky's on your list of places to visit. It is unquestionably one of the finest sources of African American cuisine in the United States.

123

DUNBAR'S FINE FOOD

Location: 4927 Freret St.
Telephone: (504) 899-0734
Proprietor: Celestine Dunbar
Dress: Casual/Classy
Menu: Soul Food
Price: Very Modest
Hours: Mon.–Sat.: 7:00 A.M.–9:00 P.M.

Comments: Dunbar's Fine Food is quickly gaining a large following in the Crescent City. Tucked away in a tiny pink building, it is decorated with a poster of the matronly Celestine Dunbar serving a heaping helping of her soulful cuisine and with photographs of the Dunbar family and visiting celebrities. The *New Orleans Tribune*, the city's African American monthly, has described the restaurant as "a New Orleans Institution." Dunbar got a late start in the restaurant business, although she has always been an entrepreneur at heart. She was operating a boutique and a beauty salon with her daughter Peggy when the owner of a nearby sandwich shop fell ill and asked Dunbar to run his place in his absence. When he recovered, he no longer wanted the business and sold it to her. The Dunbars operated the restaurant on Oak Street for two years, then opted for a better location at the current Freret Street address. Since the restaurant's modest beginnings in 1989, their business has expanded significantly. The most popular item on the menu, according to Dunbar, is the red beans and rice with fried chicken, mustard greens, and candied yams. Other local favorites include gumbo, stuffed peppers, seafood po-boys, and a spicy rice dish with liver and onions. Dunbar's husband Hillard personally prepares the popular potato salad. When you eat a meal at Dunbar's, don't forget to save room for their delicious bread pudding or walnut pound cake.

EDDIE'S RESTAURANT & BAR

Location: 2119 Law St.
Telephone: (504) 945-2207
Proprietor: Eddie Baquet, Sr.
Dress: Casual/Classy
Menu: Creole
Price: Modest
Hours: Mon.–Thurs.:
11:00 A.M.–10:00 P.M.; Fri.–Sat.: 11:00 A.M.–11:30 P.M.

Comments: Eddie Baquet, Sr., has been in the restaurant business a little more than half a century. He has been at this location since 1965. His restaurant is cozy and boasts excellent service. Actor Bill Cosby was so taken by his visit to Eddie's in the late 1970s that he was later compelled to compliment it during an interview on what was then Johnny Carson's "Tonight Show." I tried their Trout Baquet, a broiled fillet of trout garnished with crabmeat and butter-lemon sauce: simply delicious! The menu features other Creole treats such as catfish jourdain, stuffed crab, seafood platter supreme, and red beans and rice. Eddie's son Wayne now runs the family's restaurant interests. (See also Zachary's.)

125

OLIVIER'S THE CREOLE RESTAURANT

Location: 204 Decatur St.
Telephone: (504) 525-7734
Proprietor: Armand Olivier, Jr.
Menu: Creole Cuisine
Dress: Classy
Hours: Daily: 11:00 A.M.–10:00 P.M.

Comments: Olivier's is an elegant Creole restaurant located across the street from the House of Blues in the French Quarter. The restaurant's decor and theme is turn-of-the-century New Orleans: soft, earthy pastels dominated by subtle yellow and brick, regal mahogany and oak fixtures, and artwork celebrating the contributions of African Americans to the city's cultural life. The menu features classic Creole dishes such as etoufees, jambalaya, and gumbo. The Creole rabbit is both a succulent entree and a testament to Armand Olivier, Jr.'s, great-grandmother, the late Jean Doubelet Gaudet, whose Creole rabbit was the family's traditional Sunday meal in a time when the meat was as much of a staple as chicken is today. Olivier uses her special recipe to prepare a meal that has become one of the restaurant's trademarks. The rabbit is oven-braised at a low temperature for an hour. Then it is stewed another two hours in a hearty roux. The dish is served with rice pilaf or oyster dressing and covered with more of its special roux. Another item from the menu is a fantastic seafood smorgasbord called Tasters Platter. It includes seafood delicacies such as deep-fried fish fillets, shrimp, oysters, Creole gumbo, stuffed crab, and salad. The music you'll often hear in the background is traditional New Orleans jazz played by the legendary clarinetist Sydney Bechet, a pioneer in bringing jazz to an international audience. His great-grandnephews Armand Olivier III and Terrence Bechet are the restaurant's managers. You'll also find paintings by Ron Bechet, an ultra-realist and Terrence's brother, hanging in the dining room. Armand Junior and his brother Milton lend their expertise behind the scenes, and Armand Junior's wife Caeryl, the matriarch of the restaurant, oversees the kitchen. Don't miss an opportunity to stop by and sample some of their outstanding cuisine and good old-fashioned Southern hospitality.

THE PRALINE CONNECTION

Location: 542 Frenchman St.
Telephone: (504) 943-3934
Proprietor: Cecil Kaigler and Curtis Moore
Dress: Casual/Classy
Menu: Creole/Soul Food/Cajun
Price: Modest
Hours: Mon.–Thurs.: 7:00 A.M.–10:00 P.M.;
Fri.–Sat.: 7:00 A.M.–2:00 A.M.; Sun.: 7:00 A.M.–6:00 P.M.

Comments: The Praline Connection is the most exciting new soul-food restaurant to arrive on the New Orleans scene in recent years. The response since its 1990 grand opening has been overwhelming. The dining room is reminiscent of a French cafe, with waiters and waitresses attired in black pants, white shirts, and derby hats. The service is Southern hospitality at its best, and the cuisine rates among the city's finest. The smothered pork chops, red beans and rice, collards, and cornbread are mouthwatering. Additional items from their outstanding menu include crawfish or shrimp etoufee, jambalaya, fried, baked, or stewed chicken, and mustard and collard greens. The cheesecake with praline sauce highlights a list of delicious desserts. You also must try the praline candy and other treats available in their candy store adjacent to the dining room. Cecil Kaigler and Curtis Moore spent many coffee breaks during their nearly 18 years at the BP Company, dreaming of opening their own restaurant. After two failed ventures, their third met with success. The Praline Connection has garnered numerous awards and has been featured in local, national, and international publications: the *New Orleans Daily*, the *Times-Picayune*, *Elle* magazine, the *New York Times*, and *Bon Appetit*, to name a few. A graduate of Southern University, Curtis Moore was honored by the U. S. Small Business Association as the Minority Small Business Advocate of the Year. The business has been featured in *Black Enterprise* magazine as one of the model small business ventures in the country and listed as one of the top 100 places to eat in America by *Money Magazine*. *New Orleans Magazine* selected the restaurant as the "Readers Choice" favorite for soul-food cuisine in 1993 and 1994. The Praline Connection also does a bustling catering business. Don't miss The Praline Connection.

ZACHARY'S

Location: 8400 Oak St.
Telephone: (504) 865-1559
Proprietor: Wayne Baquet, Jr.
Dress: Classy
Menu: Creole
Price: Moderate
Hours: Mon.–Thurs.: 11:00 A.M.–2:30 P.M., 5:30 P.M.–9:30 P.M.;
Fri.: 11:30 A.M.–2:30 P.M., 5:30 P.M.–10:00 P.M.;
Sat.: 5:30 P.M.–10:00 P.M.

Comments: In 1984, Wayne Baquet took over the Baquet family's restaurant interests, which include their first restaurant, the popular Eddie's mentioned earlier, an eatery on Canal Street, and Zachary's, their most upscale venture to date. Zachary's is located near Loyola University in a quiet community and a beautiful peach-and-rose building trimmed in sea blue that dates to the late 1800s. The main dining room features elegant peach-and-mauve floral tablecloths against a white backdrop. A second dining room called the Jazz Room is bathed in peach and accented by lithographs of jazz legends Louis Armstrong and Miles Davis. The menu is highlighted by an attractive array of Creole cuisine such as crabmeat au gratin and "Kelly's seafood platter... served with jumbo shrimp, oysters, stuffed crab, catfish, and a crawfish pie." From the grill, they offer ribeye steaks, veal, and pork chops. Chef's specials include Southern fried chicken and roast beef brisket. The Baquet family not only has solid roots in the restaurant business, they also trace their heritage back to the very foundations of jazz in America. When you enter the restaurant, take a moment to look at the display case on the right wall. You'll learn that Theogene Baquet, a cornetist, founded the Excelsior Brass Band in the late 1800s. His son Achille recorded with the original Dixieland Jazz Band while another son, clarinetist George Baquet, played with Buddy Bolden, generally regarded as the founder of jazz, in the early 1900s. The latter Baquet also played and recorded with jazz legends Willie "Bunk" Johnson, Papa Celestin, and Jelly Roll Morton. The restaurant's namesake is the senior Baquet's grandson, Zachary. Reservations are generally not required, except for parties of ten or more. Make this one of your top considerations for dinner.

DANCING

THE BOTTOM LINE

Location: 2101 N. Claiborne Ave.
Telephone: (504) 947-9297
Clientele: Mature/Young Adult
Format: R & B/Top 40
Calendar: Dancing Nightly
Cover/Minimum: Yes/No
Dress: Classy

Comments: The Bottom Line is one of the longest-running African American-owned clubs in New Orleans, and many of its patrons are fiercely loyal to the club for that very reason. This three-story establishment has the atmosphere of a house party. Its clientele represents every facet of the city's economic and social structure, university professors and taxi drivers alike, and the rhythms of the city are captured within its walls. Lester Johnson founded The Bottom Line during the early 1960s, and an evening here is like a journey back in time. The Bottom Line offers great entertainment and a chance to meet residents from all parts of town.

129

CITY LIGHTS

Location: 310 Howard Ave.
Telephone: (504) 568-1702
Clientele: Young/Mature Adult
Format: Top 40
Calendar: Dancing Wed.–Sat.
Cover/Minimum: Yes/No
Dress: Classy

Comments: City Lights is the most upscale disco in downtown New Orleans. Its elaborate light shows and sound system are interwoven to create an atmosphere of continuous excitement. A club spokesman said that any celebrity who visits the Crescent City is likely to stop here. Some of the notable guests have included "Soul Train" host Don Cornelius, comedienne Joan Rivers, and numerous NFL stars. Entertainers who have performed here include Chubby Checker, Sam Moore of Sam and Dave, and Martha and the Vandellas.

CLUB WHISPERS

Location: 8700 Lake Forest Blvd.
Telephone: (504) 245-1059
Clientele: Young Adult
Format: Top 40/R & B/House
Calendar: Dancing Tues.–Sat.
Cover/Minimum: Yes/No
Dress: Classy

Comments: This is one of the most popular R & B clubs in New Orleans. It has a big dance floor, abundant seating, and two large octagonal bars. Club Whispers is decorated in light pastels accentuated by soft lighting to add a tropical touch. The music pulsates from an elaborate sound system that provides a compelling invitation to dance.

131

RALEIGH-DURHAM, NO. CAROLINA

Chapel Hill, Durham, and Raleigh comprise what has become widely known as the Research Triangle due to the large number of research facilities in the area. Each city has a major university: the University of North Carolina, Duke University, and North Carolina State University respectively. This region also includes a number of "traditionally black colleges": Shaw University and St. Augustine College in Raleigh, North Carolina Central University in Durham, and North Carolina A. & T. in nearby Greensboro.

It was in Greensboro at a Woolworth lunch counter in 1960 that North Carolina A. & T. students sat at a "white only" counter and were denied service. News of their refusal to move spread throughout the city and, within 24 hours, throughout the nation as well. This single act of defiance gave rise to other sit-ins by university students all over the South, which, like Montgomery's bus boycotts, were one of the key planks of the Civil Rights movement.

Unique to the region is the style of blues known as Piedmont, where the music was lighter and less plaintive than early Delta blues. During the 1930s and 1940s, musicians such as Blind Gary Davis, Walter Brown McGhee (Blind Boy Fuller), Blind Sonny Terry, Bull City Red, and the Trice Brothers (Richard and William) were at the forefront of what has been characterized as the Piedmont style. Like many blues men, Blind Boy Fuller, originally from Knoxville, Tennessee, traveled as a hobo throughout the South. He worked the streets and juke joints of Durham, teaming with Sonny Terry of Greensboro, Georgia. The late Mary Lou Williams is one of the area's most-revered jazz artists. Her compositions between 1939 and 1953 parallel the evolution of jazz, ranging from swing to bebop. Other great area musicians include the late pianist and innovator of modern jazz Thelonious Monk, from Rocky Mount, and legendary saxophonist Charlie Parker, from Hamlet.

A good source of information on African American contributions to the region is Durham's historic St. Joseph's AME Church, site of the Hayti Heritage Center. The center houses a national archives and galleries of memorabilia. Whether you are visiting one of the many area colleges or just taking a weekend jaunt, the Triangle area is full of history and teeming with attrac

MUSIC

BERKELEY CAFE

Location: 217 W. Martin St.

Telephone: (919) 821-0777

Clientele: Young/Mature Adult

Format: Rock/Blues/R & B

Calendar: Live Entertainment Tues. & Thurs.–Sat.

Cover/Minimum: Yes/No

Dress: Casual

Comments: Consistent booking of top-notch regional and national talent has garnered Berkeley Cafe the position of preeminent blues room in the Triangle area. The club had modest beginnings, opening originally as a lunch place in 1984. Local lore has it that an aspiring musician stopped by one day, liked the feel of the cafe, and asked if he could play the room. The management agreed, and the Pigz Brothers became a top local blues draw while the cafe found a niche as a blues room. Over the years, owner John Blomquist has expanded the house format to a venue where local acts are the norm during the week, touring acts on weekends. Blues and R & B standout Larry Hutcherson heads the list of local favorites. Tinsley Ellis, "Steady Rollin'" Bob Margolin, the Nighthawks, and Jimmy Thackery are among the touring acts who have performed. The Berkeley also plays host to the annual Artsplosure, a celebration that brings together top blues acts representing the indigenous Piedmont blues and touring acts from across the country. Somewhat sparse on decor, Berkeley Cafe definitely has the ambience typical of the more successful blues venues. Original brick and mortar date to the 1930s when the building housed a drugstore. The club consists of three rooms, the first with a small sit-down bar on the right and a row of hardwood booths. The main room includes a long sit-down bar on the right, several high cocktail tables, and a small dance floor just in front of the stage. Another room in the rear holds a pool table and pinball machines. The restaurant opens Monday through Friday for lunch from 11:00 A.M. until 3:00 P.M., then reopens at 6:00 P.M. on nights when entertainment is featured. Berkeley burgers are the most popular item from the menu. Ribeye steaks and Greek and Cajun chicken salads also are popular orders. Sets usually begin about 10:00 P.M.

133

CAPPER'S RESTAURANT & TAVERN

Location: 4421 Six Forks Rd.
Telephone: (919) 787-8963
Clientele: Young/Mature Adult
Format: Jazz/Blues/R & B
Calendar: Live Entertainment Nightly
Cover/Minimum: No/No
Dress: Classy

Comments: Capper's unfailingly has been voted the Triangle's top jazz club by an annual public opinion poll in the *Spectator*, a local weekly guide. The room is elegant and cozy. A series of shelves line the walls, each filled with large white mugs bearing the nicknames of longtime patrons. Tradition has it that the mug must sport a sobriquet such as "Bumble Bee" or "Windy's Sister"; a simple surname won't suffice. Saxophonist Ira Wiggins is one of the club's most popular jazz performers. As director of music at North Carolina Central University, he is famous for bringing in visiting musicians and turning his performances into hot jam sessions. Vocalist Nnenna Freelon and local recording star and guitarist Scott Sawyer also have strong followings. Skeeter Brandon and Highway 61 and Norfolk's Useless Playboys have been among the most popular blues acts. While most seats provide excellent views of the band, the middle of the dining room is always good. This is especially true on nights when the music is so inviting that patrons convince the management to push aside tables in front of the stage so they can dance. John Kilgore founded Capper's Restaurant & Tavern in 1987. In 1993, Kilgore sold Capper's to two friends, Keith Fogelman and Karl Ritz. Avid fisherman, they supply Capper's with fresh catch, such as yellow-fin and blue-fin tuna, that often is not available in other restaurants. One of Chef Guy Branaman's specialties, Bayou Teche, consists of shrimp and scallops sauteed in a thick Cajun roux and served in a spicy, deep-fried eggplant "boat." The restaurant maintains a list of customers who insist on being called whenever this dish is prepared. Capper's is open for lunch from 11:00 A.M. Monday through Friday and for dinner from 5:00 P.M. Monday through Saturday. Reservations are encouraged Monday through Thursday, then it's first come, first served. This should be among your top choices for jazz and fine dining in the Triangle area.

134

42ND STREET OYSTER BAR

Location: 507 W. Jones St.
Telephone: (919) 831-2811
Clientele: Young/Mature Adult
Format: Blues/Jazz/R & B
Calendar: Live Entertainment Thurs.–Sat.
Cover/Minimum: No/No
Dress: Casual/Classy

Comments: The 42nd Street Oyster Bar is a beautiful seafood restaurant and club located on the edge of downtown Raleigh. The cozy environs of the restaurant combine Old World charm with a nautical theme. Replicas of Atlantic fish decorate the walls. The right side of the dining room is lined with hardwood booths and tables draped with white linen cloth. Period photographs dating back to the 1920s, including a life-size mural in the front of the dining room, depict Carolina life as it once was. A display on the wall next to the entrance reads "Famous North Carolina Politicians that have eaten at 42nd St. Oyster Bar." Below it are placards numbered one through thirteen, a hierarchy representing the incumbent governor and two past governors through the house speaker pro tem. The oyster bar circumnavigates the edge of the dining room. The bar has little table extensions spaced about four feet apart, each having just enough room for a party of four. On the other side of the bar, the kitchen is in full view, bustling with activity. The restaurant seats more than 200. The band plays on a portable platform near the sit-down bar on the opposite side of the dining room. Skeeter Brandon and Highway 61 head the list of top-flight local blues acts who have performed here. Tables and booths at the far end of the dining room offer a limited view of the band; however, speakers all around the room keep the music close. An order of spicy steamed shrimp comes with hush puppies, cole slaw, and sauce. Oysters on the half shell, fried frog legs, snow-crab legs, North Carolina catfish (fried, blackened, or mesquite grilled), and lobster tail are some of the specials available, all served with cole slaw or salad and a choice of potato. You'll also want to try their key lime pie, made fresh daily. The restaurant fills quickly on weekends after 6:00 P.M. Shows begin around 10:00 P.M. Reservations are accepted for the dining room. Make them well in advance for parties of seven or more.

GWENDOLYN'S INC.

Location: 1607 Curtis Dr.
Telephone: (919) 828-4418
Clientele: Mature Adult
Format: Blues/Jazz/R & B
Calendar: Live Entertainment Thurs. & Sun.; Dancing Fri.–Sat.
Cover/Minimum: Yes/No
Dress: Classy

Comments: Gwendolyn's is an attractive club located in downtown Raleigh. Founded by Gwendolyn Dozier in 1989, the club has garnered a strong and loyal following with its consistent mix of blues, jazz, and R & B. Maurice Wynn, the Triangle's one-man blues band (guitar, keyboard, and vocals), has been packing the house every Thursday night since the club's grand opening. A line-up of artists from Durham includes Jerry White and the Elite Band. Stanley Baird and Sweet Dreams can be heard each Sunday playing a range of music from straightahead jazz to R & B. This two-story club is decorated in black and gold upstairs with low-slung cocktail tables. Downstairs, the ambience is quite a bit different, with mauve accents throughout and high cocktail tables. The entire club has a capacity of 350. Gwendolyn's has a private membership format; however, tell them at the door that you are an out-of-town guest or a first-time visitor, and they will show you around the club and give you a temporary membership for the evening. Be sure to stop by when you're visiting the Triangle. Thursday shows are an absolute must experience.

IRREGARDLESS CAFE

Location: 901 W. Morgan St.
Telephone: (919) 833-8898
Clientele: Young/Mature Adult
Format: Jazz
Calendar: Live Entertainment Varies
Cover/Minimum: No/No
Dress: Casual/Classy

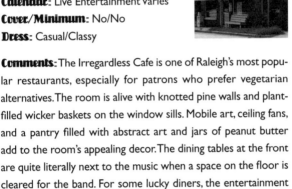

Comments: The Irregardless Cafe is one of Raleigh's most popular restaurants, especially for patrons who prefer vegetarian alternatives. The room is alive with knotted pine walls and plant-filled wicker baskets on the window sills. Mobile art, ceiling fans, and a pantry filled with abstract art and jars of peanut butter add to the room's appealing decor. The dining tables at the front are quite literally next to the music when a space on the floor is cleared for the band. For some lucky diners, the entertainment is tableside. The music is jazz, rather on the light side of acoustic, but enjoyable nonetheless. Pat Polanski on piano and Gayle Kenny on bass, comprising a duo called Jazz Impromptwo, are regularly featured. Arthur, Sanford, Barbara, and Ruth Gordon boast the freshest menu in town, a selection of ever-changing offerings that are the result of daily forays to the market for produce. Their Vegetarian Shepherd's Pie is "a hearty casserole baked in layers of mashed potatoes, cabbage sour cream saute, fresh spinach, honey carrots, corn, peas, and shortcrust pastry topping." Paella, tuna Kilamanjaro, and Mediterranean chicken are among the international favorites that have been produced by the kitchen. As of this writing, Irregardless Cafe is recovering from a fire that damaged the rear of the building in June 1994. My experience has been that it often takes from four to six months for a place to settle the insurance claim, remodel, and reopen after a fire. Give them a call when you're in the city. This intimate and attractive place is well worth a visit.

SELDOM BLUES CAFE

Location: 206-B New Waverly Place (Cary, N.C.)
Telephone: (919) 851-2583
Clientele: Young/Mature Adult
Format: Blues/Jazz/R & B
Calendar: Live Entertainment Tues.–Sat.
Cover/Minimum: No/No (Expect
cover for selected national acts)
Dress: Classy

Comments: Seldom Blues is the most striking entertainment venue in the Triangle; moreover, its facade and ambience have few peers in the Southeast. Like Miami's Amnesia, Pine Bluff's PJ's Disco, and Nashville's Malibu Beach, Seldom Blues is notable for its sheer beauty and imaginative design. Interior designer Darryl Davis incorporated some of the elements he observed in clubs throughout the East Coast to achieve a startling pastel decor. Glass-block columns containing pink lights suffuse the main dining room with a warm glow. A horseshoe-shaped bar with a dark marble top is mounted on pink tile against a charcoal backdrop. A white baby grand piano above the bar is adjacent to a small dance floor bathed in black granite. The most-coveted seats in the dining room are on the second floor, in a little alcove that curves out above the main floor. Seats along the rail on the second floor also provide an unrestricted view of the performers from above. A second room features a similar decor, but in a smaller, more intimate setting. The two rooms seat 230 and 85 respectively. R & B and blues virtuoso Will Silver is one of the most popular local draws. Terry Garland was a big hit with his hot offering of Bayou blues. Although the emphasis consistently has centered upon local artists, the club's booking strategy is evolving towards a larger mix of regional and national acts. Seldom Blues has been featured in the *Atlanta Constitution* and the local weekly guide, the *Spectator,* as the city's top blues venue. A menu of continental, seafood, and pasta dishes also provides a compelling reason to include Seldom Blues as a must experience when visiting the Triangle area. The restaurant begins serving at 5:30 P.M. Entertainment starts at 7:00 P.M. during the week and at 8:00 P.M. on weekends (when reservations are highly encouraged).

DINING

MAE'S COUNTRY KITCHEN

Location: 610 W. South St.
Telephone: (919) 821-5884
Menu: Southern
Dress: Casual/Classy
Price: Very Modest
Hours: Mon.–Fri.: 6:00 A.M.–2:30 P.M.; Sat.: 7:30 A.M.–12:30 P.M.

Comments: Mae's Country Kitchen is a tiny eatery located several blocks south of Shaw University and downtown Raleigh. Gray brick, cedar panels, and a long, L-shaped serving counter dominate the room's decor. Several booths line the wall opposite the lunch counter. Around midday, the place is bustling with patrons who come by for take-out or grab a booth or a stool at the counter, barely able to contain themselves at the prospect of Mae's down-home offerings. She features a special each day. On my first visit, it happened to be a heaping plate full of fried pork chops, a choice of two vegetables (I chose steamed cabbage and turnip greens), two wedges of cornbread, a large glass of iced tea, and a slice of orange pound cake. At $4.79, it's easy to understand why the lines are so long. These customers know value! They come in all sorts, from doctors to postal carriers. Students and faculty members of Shaw University also number among Mae's clientele. Other items from the menu range from entrees such as stew beef and fried chicken liver and gizzards to an assortment of veggies such as black-eyed peas, fresh butter beans, and red beets. The homemade lemon pie, apple cobbler, and pound cake also are special treats. Mae Perry has been at this location since 1991, but she has logged more than 30 years in the restaurant business, having previously cooked in area hotels and restaurants. Her Country Kitchen is her initial venture as an entrepreneur. Her husband Louis, sons Cedric, Conley, and Kenneth, and daughters Lena and Vivian each lend a hand in making the restaurant successful. Even with the demands of running a business, Mae Perry also finds time to team with Ethel Elliott to form the gospel duet, the Branchettes, performing at area churches and for local civic functions. Stop by, sit down or grab a take-out, and enjoy!

DANCING

TAJ MAHAL

Location: 325 Tryon Rd.
Telephone: (919) 772-1249
Clientele: Young/Mature Adult
Format: R & B/House
Calendar: Live Entertainment Varies; Dancing Fri.–Sat.
Cover/Minimum: Yes/No
Dress: Classy

Comments: Taj Mahal boasts the largest dance floor in North Carolina. A large, circular bar sits in the middle of the room, ringed by a gigantic hardwood dance floor, which in turn is ringed by concentric circles of cocktail tables. Four pairs of audio speakers are suspended around the dance floor. A stage on the right side of the room, as one enters, accommodates even the largest of acts. Two photography stations for patrons who want to capture their visit on film are poised against scenic backdrops at the rear of the club. The entire complex covers 35,000 square feet. Conservative estimates put the club's capacity at more than 4,800, while the dance floor is said to hold more than 300. Just opened in the spring of 1994, Taj Mahal has already emerged as one of the top dance spots in the Carolinas. The club features touring acts monthly. DJ Flex, Aaron Hall, the Manhattans, and CeCe Penniston are some of the top acts booked thus far. The club also has launched two comedy talent searches, a venue they hope to install semi-annually. A visit to Taj Mahal guarantees an evening at one of the Southeast's largest dance parties.

140

MUSIC

COACH'S CORNER

Location: 2510 University Dr.
Telephone: (919) 490-3006
Clientele: Young Adult
Format: Blues/Southern Rock
Calendar: Live Entertainment Fri. or Sat.
Cover/Minimum: Yes/No
Dress: Casual

Comments: The Coach's Corner is a striking gray building with blue awnings and a hardwood patio. A sign above the door reads "Duke." The white ceiling, the blue walls, and the Duke sports memorabilia throughout make the point very clearly—this is Blue Devil country. Four dart boards located around the room underscore another preoccupation of patrons who stop by. In fact, the Coach's Corner features a darts tournament each Tuesday. On weekends, the pool table and the eight dining tables are pushed aside to accommodate the crowds who come out to hear live blues and rock & roll. Rockin' Rye plays a combination of both, while Jessie's Zoo is more known for Southern rock. Whereas seating can handle about 40, standing room bulges up to 80. The outdoor patio is equipped with speakers to accommodate overflow crowds. Burgers, grilled chicken sandwiches, and steamed shrimp are the main draws from the menu. This sports bar is open Monday through Saturday from 4:00 P.M. and Sunday from noon. As one can imagine, this is one of Durham's hottest spots during football and basketball season.

THE PALACE INTERNATIONAL

Location: 117 W. Parrish St.
Telephone: (919) 687-4922
Clientele: Young Adult
Format: World Beat/Reggae/Salsa/R & B
Calendar: Live Entertainment Fri.; Dancing Fri.–Sat.
Cover/Minimum: Yes/No
Dress: Casual

Comments: The Palace International is a large, cavernous club located in the middle of downtown Durham. A long, S-shaped bar courses through the front lounge area where seating accommodates about 40. A flight of steps leads down to the first of two entertainment venues, and cocktail seating in a mezzanine on the right overlooks a large, checkerboard-tile dance floor. An elevated stage is located at the rear of the dance floor. This is the venue for African, Caribbean, and world beat music as well as for live performances. Another flight of steps from here leads down to the basement level where patrons can find R & B, hip hop, and house music, spun by one of Durham's cadre of local deejays. The booking philosophy of The Palace International is local, regional, and international in scope. Zairian Soukous artists Taboulay, Mbila-Abel, and Petekale; Trinidad calypso star Mighty Sparrow; soca standout Arrow; and Nigeria's Shina Peters performing high life, a popular West African dance music, have all been featured. The regional acts have included reggae artists Uprising of Baltimore and Awareness Art Ensemble of Richmond. Chapel Hill's Majestic Lions head the list of local acts who have performed. The Palace features lunch daily from 11:00 A.M. until 4:00 P.M. The focal point of the menu is East African cuisine from the coastal region, with such offerings as Nairobi beef, chicken Karunga, and Dengu n' Chapati, a bread made with flour and lentils cooked in coconut milk and spices. Samousas are the most popular appetizers. Maurice and Caren Ochola, native-born Kenyans, opened this club and restaurant in 1988. The Ocholas also do a bustling catering business on the campuses of these schools and in many area homes. This club has become one of Durham's bedrock institutions and, as of this writing, employs one of the most impressive booking strategies in the Triangle area.

TALK OF THE TOWN

Location: 198 E. Main St.
Telephone: (919) 682-7747
Clientele: Young/Mature Adult
Format: Jazz/R & B/Blues
Calendar: Live Entertainment Thurs.–Sat.
Cover/Minimum: Yes/No
Dress: Classy

Comments: The Talk of the Town is one of the Triangle's most consistent jazz, R & B, and blues venues. The long, rectangular room is elegant and cozy. Shaped somewhat like a trapezoid, a stately white-oak bar trimmed in green leather sits on the left side of the restaurant. A green leather couch built into the right wall spans half the dining room. The restaurant is a favorite lunch-time stop for many of the city's businessmen and women. Beginning each Thursday, the tables are pushed back to accommodate a large dance floor in the rear, just in front of the bandstand, making the transition from elegant restaurant to jazz supper club in the blink of an eye. Sam and Audrey Sellers owned the Talk Of the Town nightclub in Brooklyn, New York, during the mid-1970s and into the late 1980s. In 1991, they moved the entire operation to Durham, to the Triangle's immense gain. The booking philosophy is decidedly local. However, many of these artists are reaching out to a regional audience. Blues and R & B standout Stanley Baird is recording on the Esquire label, while Roy Roberts, another local favorite, is also negotiating a record deal. Other popular acts include Sweet Dreams, j.b. and Friends, and Johnny White, all of whom play a mix of blues, jazz, and R & B. One-man blues band Maurice Wynn is another local artist to be reckoned with. Audrey Sellers doubles as head chef, preparing a menu that includes platters of fried fish, grilled chicken, grilled ribeye, and veggies in season. The platters come with Idaho fries, cole slaw or potato salad, and hushpuppies. The Talk Of The Town has been featured as the city's best in the *Herald Sun*, a daily, the *Independent*, a news weekly, the *Spectator*, an entertainment weekly, and in most of the area entertainment guides. They are open for lunch Tuesday through Friday from 11:00 A.M. and for dinner Thursday through Saturday from 6:00 P.M.

DINING

DILLARD'S

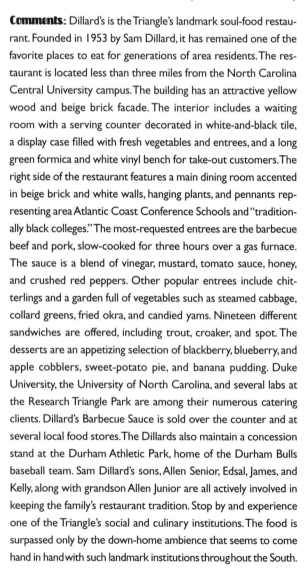

Location: 3921 Fayetteville St.
Telephone: (919) 544-1587
Menu: Soul Food/Barbecue
Dress: Casual/Classy
Price: Very Modest
Hours: Mon.–Sat.: 7:00 A.M.–9:00 P.M. (until 10:00 P.M. on Fri.)

Comments: Dillard's is the Triangle's landmark soul-food restaurant. Founded in 1953 by Sam Dillard, it has remained one of the favorite places to eat for generations of area residents. The restaurant is located less than three miles from the North Carolina Central University campus. The building has an attractive yellow wood and beige brick facade. The interior includes a waiting room with a serving counter decorated in white-and-black tile, a display case filled with fresh vegetables and entrees, and a long green formica and white vinyl bench for take-out customers. The right side of the restaurant features a main dining room accented in beige brick and white walls, hanging plants, and pennants representing area Atlantic Coast Conference Schools and "traditionally black colleges." The most-requested entrees are the barbecue beef and pork, slow-cooked for three hours over a gas furnace. The sauce is a blend of vinegar, mustard, tomato sauce, honey, and crushed red peppers. Other popular entrees include chitterlings and a garden full of vegetables such as steamed cabbage, collard greens, fried okra, and candied yams. Nineteen different sandwiches are offered, including trout, croaker, and spot. The desserts are an appetizing selection of blackberry, blueberry, and apple cobblers, sweet-potato pie, and banana pudding. Duke University, the University of North Carolina, and several labs at the Research Triangle Park are among their numerous catering clients. Dillard's Barbecue Sauce is sold over the counter and at several local food stores. The Dillards also maintain a concession stand at the Durham Athletic Park, home of the Durham Bulls baseball team. Sam Dillard's sons, Allen Senior, Edsal, James, and Kelly, along with grandson Allen Junior are all actively involved in keeping the family's restaurant tradition. Stop by and experience one of the Triangle's social and culinary institutions. The food is surpassed only by the down-home ambience that seems to come hand in hand with such landmark institutions throughout the South.

MUSIC

THE ISLANDS

Location: 159 1/2 E. Franklin St.
Telephone: (919) 933-8332
Clientele: Young Adult
Format: Reggae/Rock/Alternative
Calendar: Live Entertainment Tues.–Sun.
Cover/Minimum: Yes/No
Dress: Casual

Comments: Don't bring mom; in fact, leave dad home as well. They won't understand. This is a typical college haunt in a town that is the prototype for college towns. The Islands, formerly Jamaica Willie's, is a bohemian sort of club located in an alley beneath The Players Club. The club has two main rooms. The first, nearest the door, is filled with wooden benches and time-worn chairs. The second room, where the band performs, is bare except for a pool table and an eclectic mural on the far wall. Reggae is the main venue on most Friday and Saturday nights. King Ayoola's reggae dance-hall music is one of the main attractions. The Hear and Now plays rockabilly on some evenings, while DSF Earth has been a regular rock & roll feature.

145

PYEWACKET RESTAURANT AND BAR

Location: 431 W. Franklin St.
Telephone: (919) 929-0297
Clientele: Young/Mature Adult
Format: Blues/Jazz
Calendar: Live Entertainment
Mon., Wed.–Thurs.
Cover/Minimum: No/No
Dress: Casual/Classy

Comments: The Pyewacket Restaurant and Bar is one of Chapel Hill's most popular dining spots. It also is one of the best places in the city to consistently hear jazz and blues. The restaurant is located in an attractive red brick building surrounded by shrubs and hedges. One of the favorite areas for patrons is a patio in front. The interior is elegantly decorated with peach and green accents throughout. Mahogany and oak, brass rails, and etched glass are the main theme in the front bar and dining area. A passageway beyond the main bar and three other dining areas comprise the remainder of the restaurant. The rear dining area is encased in smoked glass. Paintings by local artists and prints by masters such as Marc Chagall and Claude Monet round out the ambience. The entire complex seats 175. During the early 1980s, the Pyewacket hosted a number of touring blues and jazz acts. The current booking philosophy emphasizes the wealth of talent on the local scene headed by an area duo performing jazz and blues favorites, Carter Minor and Scott Sawyer on vocals/harmonica and guitar respectively. Pyewacket is best known for its seafood and vegetarian menu. Their excellent grilled salmon is sauteed with shallot butter and cracked peppercorns. One of the most popular vegetarian entrees is the Indonesian curry vegetables served over brown rice. A line-up of delicious desserts is highlighted by their black-bottom pie, a rich chocolate custard topped with whipped cream and pecan bits. The menu and the music provide excellent reasons to consider this among your top choices when visiting the Triangle area.

DINING

DIP'S

Location: 405 W. Rosemary St.
Telephone: (919) 942-5837
Proprietor: Mildred "Dip" Council
Menu: Southern
Dress: Casual/Classy
Price: Very Modest
Hours: Mon.–Fri.: 8:00 A.M.–3:00 P.M.; 4:00 P.M.–10:00 P.M.;
Sat.: 8:00 A.M.–10:00 P.M.; Sun.: 8:00 A.M.–9:00 P.M.

Comments: Dip's is one of the most attractive soul-food places in the Triangle. The restaurant is all earth tones, old brick and mortar, and cedar paneling. On the countertop, a wicker display case is lined with jars of Mama Dip's Poppy Seed Dressing and Mama Dip's Bar-B-Que Sauce. Five sets of booths, all hardwood and black leather, line the far wall of the main dining room on the right. The picture windows look out onto a stand of trees, giving the illusion of dining at grandma's house and, afterwards, sitting out on the veranda. According to Mama Dip's granddaughter Cissy, the barbecue ribs and the lightly battered fried chicken are the most-requested entrees. The Country Breakfast includes staples such as salmon cake, chicken and gravy, country ham, and eggs, all served with a choice of grits or hashbrowns and piping hot biscuits or toast. Additional entrees include combination plates with barbecue chicken and ribs, chopped barbecue with chicken, and Brunswick stew and barbecue chicken and dumplings. A tantalizing array of desserts such as pecan, apple, and sweet-potato pies; German chocolate, lemon and orange pound, and coconut cakes; and peach and apple cobblers also are too good to pass up. Mildred Council has been in this location almost 18 years. She originally started with a small restaurant. Over the years, its popularity grew, and she purchased the adjacent property, had one wall knocked out, and created the country-inn ambience the restaurant enjoys today. It seats about 80 diners. Council's barbecue sauce is a tomato-based recipe that dates back to 1957. Daughters Elaine and Spring and son Joe are each actively involved in the restaurant. So is a third generation, represented by grandchildren Cissy, Sherry, and Tonya. Stop by and experience down-home ambience, Southern hospitality, and outstanding Southern cuisine.

DINING

SCOTT'S BAR-B-QUE

Location: 1201 N. William St.
Telephone: (919) 734-0711
Proprietor: A. Martel Scott, Jr.
Menu: Barbecue/Seafood
Dress: Casual/Classy
Price: Very Modest
Hours: Tues.–Sat. 11:00 A.M.–7:00 P.M.

Comments: Adam Scott started the family barbecue tradition in 1917 when he cooked barbecue out of his home and achieved such popularity that he became known as the king of eastern North Carolina barbecue. Scott taught his son, A. Martel Senior, the fine points of the business, and the pair's fame spread as far as the White House where they prepared North Carolina barbecue for President Franklin D. Roosevelt. Martel Senior and his wife Ann operated similarly out of their home during the early 1940s. In 1952, they opted for a restaurant in the current location. On the wall behind the cashier is an autographed photograph of former President George Bush. All of the Republican presidents dating back to Gerald Ford either called or wrote letters of condolence when they heard news of Martel Senior's death. The family are lifelong Democrats, and Martel Junior is quick to point out the irony of their fame with Republican administrations. Martel Junior cites a Scott tradition of utilizing the whole pig as one of the keys to their popularity. Barbecue pork, beef, and chicken are their trademarks. Their fried chicken and seafood also are popular. A vast array of delicious pies highlight the desserts: apple, chocolate, coconut, lemon, and pecan. Scott describes their barbecue sauce as a noncaloric, vinegar-based sauce versatile enough to be used as a salad dressing. After Martel Junior graduated from Howard University in the early 1950s and did a stint in the U.S. Air Force, his father convinced him to come home and sell the barbecue sauce commercially. It turned out to be an excellent move. Today, they sell almost 2,000 cases per month to 25 wholesalers, 10 major chains throughout the Southeast, including Food Lion, and more than 100 restaurants. *Food & Wine Magazine* has voted them number two in the country in the category of thin, vinegar-based sauces. Put this one at the top of your list when visiting eastern North Carolina.

148

RICHMOND, VIRGINIA

Richmond residents are quick to point out that African Americans have long been among the nation's most innovative as trendsetters and developers of business enterprises. If you look at the city's history, this claim is born out by the achievements of individuals such as the Reverend William Washington Brown, a former slave who, following emancipation, founded the United Order of True Reformers in 1881. This organization, one of many benevolent societies throughout the South, was to receive a charter seven years later for the Savings Bank of the Order of True Reformers. They opened six months after the Capitol Savings Bank of Washington, D.C., which started operations in October 1888; these two institutions were the country's first African American banks. In 1903, when Maggie L. Walker was named president of Richmond's St. Luke Bank, she became the first African American woman to head a high capitalization bank.

Virginia Union, a "historically black college," was founded in 1865, just two years after the abolition of slavery. One of its graduates, Virginia State Senator Henry L. Marsh, was elected the city's first African American mayor in 1977. Dr. Roy A. West, Walter Kenney, and the Reverend Leonidas B. Young, pastor of the historic Fourth Baptist Church, followed him. Dr. West and Mayor Young also are graduates of the university. Virginia Union's L. Douglas Wilder, a grandson of former slaves, was elected Virginia's lieutenant governor in 1985 and governor in 1989, achieving distinction as the first African American elected governor in the history of the United States. Other distinguished graduates include Washington, D.C., Congressman Walter E. Fauntroy, Vice Admiral Samuel L. Gravely (Ret.), the Navy's first African American admiral, and Dr. Frank S. Royal, former president of the National Medical Association.

Richmond offers many compelling reasons to visit, foremost among them being its stunning beauty and Southern charm. Maggie Walker's home at 110 1/2 Leigh Street, the Maggie L. Walker National Historic Site, is one of two African American museums in the city. The Black History Museum and Cultural Center of Virginia, located at 00 Clay Street, also offers a wealth of information on the history of Richmond and the state.

MUSIC

BOGART'S RESTAURANT

Location: 203 N. Lombardy St.
Telephone: (804) 353-9280
Clientele: Young/Mature Adult
Format: Jazz
Calendar: Live Entertainment Fri.–Sat.
Cover/Minimum: No/No
Dress: Classy

Comments: Bogart's has been one of Richmond's finest jazz supper clubs since it opened in the early 1970s. Mark Karakas had worked in the restaurant business for most of his life, including a stint at Bogart's. When the previous owners heard that he and his wife Georgia were looking for a restaurant, they offered them the opportunity to take over Bogart's. The couple assumed ownership of the club in 1992, and it has not missed a beat. The house bands are the Joe Scott Quartet, who have developed a loyal following over the years for their sizzling renditions of R & B standards, and QED, a popular local group playing a wide range of jazz. The jazz room is located at the rear of the club. In addition to outstanding music, this room is reserved for fine dining. The menu includes a variety of seafood, beef, chicken, and pasta entrees. Bogart's also has two other dining rooms offering more casual dining and an additional menu that includes sandwiches.

150

FARMER'S MARKET INN

Location: 1707 East Franklin St.
Telephone: (804) 344-8145
Clientele: Young/Mature Adult
Format: Blues
Calendar: Live Entertainment
Thurs.–Sat.
Cover/Minimum: Yes/No
Dress: Casual/Classy

Comments: The Farmer's Market Inn is Richmond's top blues establishment. When you walk in, you'll quickly get the impression that blues is what this house is all about. While the decor doesn't feature the standard memorabilia you expect in most blues establishments, it does have the snug feel that is characteristic of many of the South's more important blues venues. This is especially evident when you catch a weekend show here. The place literally rocks as patrons respond enthusiastically to the club's usual cadre of regional and local blues bands. Many find their way to the dance floor, while others just sit back and enjoy a variety of blues that ranges from acoustic to jumpin' to Chicago style. The club has been a mainstay in Richmond for a number of years under various owners. One of the current owners, Robert McGrory, certainly knows his way around the music scene, having been a drummer in various Richmond rock bands. He and his wife Patrice, along with his sister Roseann McGrory, took over the club in late 1993. They hope to maintain The Farmer's Market Inn's blues tradition by continuing to book acts such as the Fabulous Silver Fins and the Blue Beats featuring Little Ronnie. I caught a tremendous performance by the latter during my first visit to the club. These young entrepreneurs are off to a fantastic start in the blues and restaurant business. They know their craft well, are outstanding hosts, and will provide you with a great evening of blues entertainment. The Farmer's Market Inn is also open Monday for lunch and Tuesday through Saturday for lunch and dinner. Its menu features Italian cuisine.

151

HIPPOLLO

Location: 528 N. Second St.
Telephone: (804) 648-4211
Clientele: Young/Mature Adult
Format: R & B/Blues/Gospel/Jazz
Calendar: Live Entertainment Varies
Cover/Minimum: Yes/na
Dress: Classy

Comments: The Hippollo Theater held its grand reopening in October 1993. The acts that reinaugurated this historic facility were Harold Melvin and the Blue Notes, Betty Wright, Tony Terry, and Richmond's own, the Jarmels, reunited for this one-time performance. Willie Poe, the theater's owner/operator, envisions the Hippollo as a key component in the revitalization of the city's fabled Second Street. Those who are familiar with Southern popular history will recall the Hippollo as the former Hippodrome, a landmark theater founded in 1904. The Hippodrome was one of the major stops on what came to be known as the "Chittlin' Circuit." Billie Holiday sang the blues here, Cab Calloway crooned and pranced, and James Brown packed the house on many nights. Keeping faith with this legacy, Poe plans to make the Hippollo a multifaceted entertainment venue. African American plays, comedy acts, and R & B oldies, gospel, and jazz performances will be scheduled regularly. Jerry Butler, Jean Carn, the Chi-Lites, Billy Paul, and regional favorite Roy "C" have already performed here. Poe also provides free movies each month for children in the neighboring community. Don't forget to give the Hippollo a call when visiting the city to find out what's on the calendar. If no acts are scheduled, it's still worth a stop just to see this beautiful 3,000-seat theater and get a glimpse of African American and Southern history.

LA LA CAFE AT RICK'S

Location: 1847 W. Broad St.
Telephone: (804) 359-1224
Clientele: Young/Mature Adult
Format: Jazz/Blues/Comedy
Calendar: Live Entertainment Thurs.–Sat.
Cover/Minimum: Yes/No
Dress: Casual/Classy

Comments: La La Cafe, also known as Rick's, has been a Richmond favorite since its inception in 1979. Its Friday and Saturday night jam sessions are heralded as the best in the city. Musicians from all over town stream through the door to sit in. The musicians clear an area in the front of the dining room, and the evening takes flight. The Keynotes are the featured house band. According to Rick Laszlo, when traveling notables come through the door, a buzz goes through the room, and the next instant, they're on stage performing. Such was the case when jazz stars Branford Marsalis of "The Jay Leno Show" and his father Ellis stopped by. La La Cafe reminds me of the kind of avant-garde bistro you find around many college campuses, with its abstract paintings, hanging plants, and ceiling fans. The music is what sets this cafe apart. Baritone sax player Ralph Branch and tenor sax man James Gates lead a jam session that sizzled. The restaurant menu features steaks, seafood, and pasta dishes. Lunch is served Monday through Friday from 11:00 A.M. to 3:00 P.M., and dinner is served Tuesday through Saturday from 5:00 P.M. to 2:00 A.M. If you're in the mood for nonstop, spontaneous jazz, this place is a must during any visit to Richmond.

153

DINING

DABNEYS RESTAURANT

Location: 1510 Robin Hood Rd.
Telephone: (804) 359-8126
Proprietor: The Dabney Family
Dress: Casual/Classy
Menu: Soul Food
Price: Very Modest
Hours: Mon.–Sat.: 7:00 A.M.–
9:30 P.M.; Sun.: 7:00 A.M.–8:00 P.M.

Comments: Dabneys Restaurant may have one of the more unusual locations for a soul-food eatery in the southeastern United
States. When you drive into the parking lot of the Howard
Johnson Lodge on Robin Hood Road, one of the first things to
capture your attention is the large Dabneys logo on the hotel's
facade. Taking advantage of the space provided by a major hotel
chain, Dabneys accommodates more than 120 patrons; adjacent
banquet rooms can serve even larger parties. The main dining
room is attractively decorated in soft pastels. Whether you saun-
ter over to the buffet line or order from their sit-down menu,
prepare for a meal that will have you coming back for more. I
had a virtual feast with my selection of their Southern fried
chicken, fried flounder, collard greens, and green beans. It was a
difficult choice, considering other tasty items from the menu such
as "Ercell's meatloaf," "Wheeler's homestyle baked spaghetti," and
cod fillet. It's small wonder why this establishment has captured
the hearts of many Richmond residents. By opening this first-
rate restaurant, James Dabney and his sister Ercell have realized
their childhood dream. Both have worked in the restaurant business since they were teenagers, and this is their second venture
since 1989. They closed their first restaurant at Richmond's Virginia Inn at the beginning of 1992 and opted for this location
shortly afterwards. All of the city's leaders, including Mayor
Walter Kenney, came by for their grand opening. Area churches
vie for the opportunity to host a dinner here, or simply to gather
for a delightful meal after Sunday services. The restaurant also
does a bustling catering business with an emphasis on weddings,
banquets, and holiday parties. No party is too big when you
choose Dabneys for a family or office gathering, and the food
and ambience are well worth the visit.

JOHNSON'S RESTAURANT

Location: 1802 E. Franklin St.
Telephone: (804) 648-9788
Proprietor: Myrtle Johnson
Dress: Casual/Classy
Menu: Soul Food
Price: Very Modest
Hours: Mon.–Fri.: 6:00 A.M.–1:00 P.M.;
Sat.: 6:00 A.M.–11:00 A.M.

Comments: Myrtle Johnson worked in the cafeteria of a major corporation during the mid-1960s. In 1971, she surprised her family by announcing that she was opening her own restaurant. Annie's Rib House, a well-regarded soul-food eatery, had sustained damage during the floods that ravaged the area the previous year, and its owners decided to get out of the business and offered Johnson the opportunity to take over. After securing financing for repairs, she reopened the place under the name Johnson's Restaurant. She soon discovered that running the business wasn't going to be easy. Her late husband Floyd became ill shortly afterward, but with the help of her children, she managed to keep the business afloat while tending him. Johnson's perseverance paid off as her clientele began to swell. She also sent all of her daughters to college; her son Floyd did a stint in the military and attended Virginia Commonwealth. Myrtle Johnson has much to be proud of. Her restaurant is one of the bedrocks of the Richmond community. Some of the most-requested items on Johnson's breakfast menu are salt herring and salmon cakes. Many in Richmond's downtown business district can't resist her tender, thick pork chops, meat loaf, and homemade rolls. Her apple and peach cobblers also are special treats. They don't stay open late, so get there early. You'll count a morning or early afternoon visit to Johnson's among your special memories of Richmond.

SECOND & MARSHALL SEAFOOD GRILL

Location: 318 N. Second St.
Telephone: (804) 643-6516
Proprietor: Alvona and Kevin Armstrong
Dress: Casual/Classy
Menu: Seafood/Soul Food
Price: Very Modest
Hours: Sun.–Wed.: 11:00 A.M.–6:00 P.M.;
Thurs.: 11:00 A.M.–8:00 P.M.; Fri.–Sat.: 7:00 A.M.–8:00 P.M.

Comments: Kevin Armstrong worked as a waiter in Charleston, South Carolina, when he was 13. That's when he began nurturing his dream of owning a restaurant some day. He moved to Richmond and bought a mobile kitchen in 1991. It was so successful that Armstrong was able to convert the capital from the mobile kitchen into a beautiful seafood/soul-food bistro in the heart of Richmond's historic district on Second Street. Known as the "Deuce" in the 1930s to 1960s, Second Street saw the likes of Louis Armstrong and Count Basie, who brought their fabled bands to perform. This is, in large measure, why Kevin and his wife Alvona chose the location. Kinte cloth accentuates the dining tables as well as the uniforms of the waitresses. The restaurant draws clientele from among state and municipal officials and the community at large. Items from the menu are named after famous African Americans, something Kevin came up with as a means of stimulating interest and dialogue between parents and their children when they go over the menu. The "Frederick Douglass," fried lake trout with two side dishes, is simply incredible. Other popular entrees include the "Daddy King," freshly prepared fried flounder, fried shrimp, and fried oysters served with fries, homemade cole slaw, and garlic toast, and the "W. E. B. Du Bois," barbecue baby back ribs. The grill also does a thriving catering business with a number of Virginia Commonwealth agencies prominent among their list of clients. Don't leave Richmond without visiting this very attractive bistro and sampling their outstanding menu.

SUGAR & SPICE

Location: 2116 E. Main St.
Telephone: (804) 788-4566
Proprietor: Martha Mobley
Dress: Casual
Menu: Soul Food
Price: Modest
Hours: Mon.–Thurs.: 8:00 A.M.–
4:00 P.M.; Fri.: 8:00 A.M.–9:00 P.M.

Comments: Martha Mobley's Sugar & Spice is a family affair. Her siblings, George, Henry, Joseph, Shirley, and Willie, all take turns in the kitchen. Martha does most of the baking. Her chocolate cakes, rice puddings, and sweet-potato pies are among the desserts she makes from scratch. The chitterlings are the most-requested entree. The restaurant offers a varied menu that includes fried chicken, lake trout, barbecue ribs, and liver and onions. I had an excellent meal of meat loaf, string beans, and an outstanding navy bean soup. Sugar & Spice also does a thriving catering business. Some of their biggest clients include the Richmond City Council and the local office of AT&T. Martha Mobley chose Sugar & Spice as the name of her restaurant in 1980 because of her love of baking. To be sure, her fine desserts are among the many reasons to spice up your dining choices by considering a meal here.

DANCING

CLUB Z

Location: 2001 E. Franklin St.
Telephone: (804) 783-2001
Clientele: Young Adult
Format: R & B / House / Club
Calendar: Live Entertainment Varies; Dancing Wed.–Sat.
Cover/Minimum: Yes / No
Dress: Classy

Comments: Club Z is one of Richmond's hottest new dance clubs. It advertises the largest dance floor in Richmond, and one look at the place on a Saturday evening substantiates that claim. The club accommodates 1,500 patrons. With its sophisticated sound and light systems, it's easy to see why this attractive club has achieved such popularity. The first floor showcases a large dance floor in one area and a billiard room in another. The second floor houses a dining room where the menu is soul food and the format is comedy. Items on the menu include seafood, barbecue ribs, liver and onions, and chitterlings. The Wednesday feature, College Night, is very popular among Virginia Union and Virginia Commonwealth University students. Since its grand opening in October 1993, the club has booked acts such as Kriss Kross, LL Cool J, Tony Terry, and the hot Washington, D.C. go go band, the Northeast Groovers. Stop by before 11:00 P.M., and the place is virtually empty. Come back after midnight, and you'll find lines that sometimes extend around the building. If dancing the night away is your cup of tea, do what many in Richmond do, and go down to Club Z for the biggest party in town.

158

PIER 7

Location: 5927 Midlothian Tpk.
Telephone: (804) 230-1714
Clientele: Mature Adult
Format: R & B
Calendar: Live Entertainment Wed.–Sat.; Dancing Wed.–Sun.
Cover/Minimum: Yes/No
Dress: Classy

Comments: Leroy "Bo" Jones has taught in the Richmond public school system for more than two decades. He and his brother, William "Roy," always had wanted to open their own restaurant, and they realized their dream in 1989 with the opening of Pier 7. The restaurant started out modestly, specializing in fast seafood. As their clientele grew, customers began to ask for a sit-down menu. The Jones brothers also branched out in the first year and imported live entertainment. They outgrew their original facility at 404 Westover, and in 1993, they relocated to a large and attractive building in the Southgate Mall. A spacious stage and dance floor are located at the front of the main dining room, which seats 350. Katz, their house band, has been a local favorite for a number of years. Ron Flowers, their deejay of choice, also is one of the main attractions for this supper club. The menu, boasting a variety of seafood dishes, is yet another attraction that keeps Pier 7 full of contented patrons. This is the place where the city's professional crowd comes to dance and enjoy a great meal. Former pro football players Doug Williams, Willie Lanier, and Franco Harris have each enjoyed an evening here. Stop in when you're in the area for superb entertainment and excellent seafood cuisine.

159

Washington, D.C. has long been considered the political center of the African American community. Some of the city's earliest luminaries include Frederick Douglass, abolitionist, orator, diplomat, and essayist, and Mordecai Johnson, early president of Howard University. Howard University has steadfastly produced some of the nation's most innovative leaders, theologians, and physicians. The late Thurgood Marshall went on to become the chief legal advocate of the Civil Rights movement and, ultimately, was appointed a justice of the United States Supreme Court. Andrew Young went on to serve two terms as mayor of Atlanta, Georgia, and was appointed United States ambassador to the United Nations. The late Dr. Charles Drew pioneered the development of the nation's invaluable blood plasma bank.

No place in the country offers a better opportunity to study the dynamics of the democratic process. Representative Eleanor Holmes Norton, Reverend Jesse Jackson, and Mayor Sharon Pratt Kelly are among a political vanguard that charts the course of the city. The Congressional Black Caucus is at the forefront on national issues.

The city has produced its share of legendary entertainers: Pearl Bailey, Billy Eckstine, and Edward Kennedy "Duke" Ellington, for example. From 1920 through the early 1950s, Washington's U Street was a mecca for entertainment and the arts, boasting such residents as author Langston Hughes and dancer Bill "Bojangles" Robinson.

Today, Black Entertainment Television (BET) has its headquarters here. Under the direction of its founder and president, Robert L. Johnson, this cable network now reaches more than 30 million households. WHMM, Howard University's public television station, is an important source of information on African American history, current events, and public service spots. Two National Public Radio affiliates, WPFW and the University of the District of Columbia's WDCU, offer programming that chronicles the evolution of jazz, blues, gospel, and R & B in America.

Washington has something for everyone. The monuments can keep you occupied for an entire visit. So can tours of the White House and other federal complexes. What's more, Washington's theaters and museums offer adventures in the arts and history that you'll find simply breathtaking.

MUSIC

BLUES ALLEY

Location: 1073 Wisconsin Ave. NW
Telephone: (202) 337-4141
Clientele: Mature Adult
Format: Jazz/Blues/R & B
Calendar: Live Entertainment Nightly
Cover/Minimum: Yes/Yes
(1 drink, large shows require meal)
Dress: Casual/Classy

Comments: Blues Alley is one of the premier jazz supper clubs in the United States. The building, located in the heart of Washington's famous Georgetown district, was constructed during the early 1700s and was once used by tobacco merchants as a carriage house. Founded in 1972, the club has long attracted jazz aficionados from throughout the country and abroad. Owner John Bunyan has the golden touch. This was true when he served as a vice president for Deak Perera, overseeing gold and silver operations, and it has certainly been the case with this club. From heads of state to members of Congress to the average man on the street, all are drawn to this venerable establishment. Virtually every notable jazz entertainer of the modern era has performed here. My first experience at Blues Alley came in 1983 when I was enthralled one evening by the sultry sounds of Eartha Kitt. Nancy Wilson and the late Sarah Vaughan are two other mistresses of jazz who have sung at Blues Alley. In December 1993, I had the pleasure of listening to the incomparable Wynton Marsalis. No stranger to Blues Alley, he recorded his first live album here in 1986. Dizzy Gillespie, Joe Williams, Tony Bennett, Chuck Mangione, and Maynard Ferguson are just a few of the jazz greats who have headlined. The club also has featured blues artists such as Albert Collins and Buddy Guy as well as R & B notables Harold Melvin and Jerry Butler. Whether you are at one of the tables surrounding the stage or in the rear of the room near the bar, no seat in the house is a bad one. In addition to the top-flight entertainment that is always available here, Blues Alley offers an exciting menu including a fantastic array of seafood and Creole cuisine. Blues Alley has few equals in the United States. It is truly one of Washington's most inviting attractions and a must experience during your stay here. Reservations are encouraged.

EVENING STAR JAZZ BAR

Location: 1200 19th St. NW
Telephone: (202) 785-STAR
Clientele: Mature Adult
Format: Jazz
Calendar: Live Entertainment Wed.–Sat.
Cover/Minimum: Yes/Yes (2 drinks)
Dress: Casual/Classy

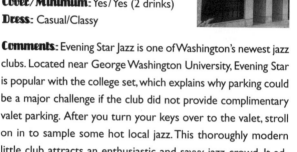

Comments: Evening Star Jazz is one of Washington's newest jazz clubs. Located near George Washington University, Evening Star is popular with the college set, which explains why parking could be a major challenge if the club did not provide complimentary valet parking. After you turn your keys over to the valet, stroll on in to sample some hot local jazz. This thoroughly modern little club attracts an enthusiastic and savvy jazz crowd. It adjoins Sam & Harry's restaurant, a popular and stylish eatery that opened in 1990. Both are owned by Michael Sternberg and Larry Work. They began holding jazz sessions in the side room in 1992. The versatile Dick Morgan is featured regularly.

162

FLEETWOOD'S RESTAURANT & BLUES CLUB

Location: 44 Canal Center Plaza (Alexandria, Va.)
Telephone: (703) 548-6425
Clientele: Young/Mature Adult
Format: Blues
Calendar: Live Entertainment Nightly
Cover/Minimum: Yes/No
Dress: Casual/Classy

Comments: Mick Fleetwood of the rock group Fleetwood Mac and Capital City Entertainment, an Alexandria-based investment and management group, opened Fleetwood's Restaurant & Blues Club on July 21, 1994. In an area where blues options are limited, their grand opening was a much-anticipated event for local fans. Fleetwood's joins a growing list of excellent large-format blues venues that are emerging around the country. Located near the trendy "Old Town" section of Alexandria, the club is one of several businesses in the Canal Center Plaza. Fleetwood's occupies two floors and has an urban, contemporary feel. Ornate floral arrangements add to the comfortable ambiance of the main room. The entire complex, including the open-air patio, accommodates more than 700. Panoramic views of the Potomac River are available throughout. If the first two months of operation are any indication, Fleetwood's Restaurant & Blues Club promises a steady helping of top-flight blues for area residents. Chuck Brown and Eva Cassidy, the Uptown Rhythm Kings, Smokin' Joe Kubek and B'nois King, Charles Brown, Bobby Parker, Kenny Neal, Junior Wells, and Big Joe and the Dynaflows already have been featured. In addition to some of the best blues artists around, the restaurant offers a versatile menu that includes hickory-grilled entrees such as salmon, prime rib, and jumbo shrimp as well as assorted pasta dishes, sandwiches, pizzas, and appetizers. The restaurant is open for lunch and dinner daily from 11:30 A.M. Most shows begin about 9:00 P.M. However, getting there by 7:00 P.M. on weekends provides the best chance of getting a table. Reservations are only accepted for parties of 20 or more. Adding to Fleetwood's attractiveness is an underground garage with an entrance leading directly into the club. Be sure to take your ticket stub inside where the club will validate it for free parking, something of a rarity in the Washington area.

GEORGIA BROWN'S

Location: 950 15th St. NW
Telephone: (202) 393-4499
Clientele: Young/Mature Adult
Format: Blues
Calendar: Live Entertainment Sunday Brunch
Cover/Minimum: No/Yes (1 drink)
Dress: Classy

Comments: Georgia Brown's is a swank new supper club in the heart of downtown Washington. Their concept brings the blues to one of the more elegant settings you'll find anywhere. The owners have taken great care to achieve a beautiful interior by commissioning one of the area's top designers, Adam Tifany, to create a dining room with flowing lines, discreet private alcoves, and soft pastels. A sculpture that reminds one of a canopy sprawls along the ceiling, creating the illusion of magnolia trees and hanging moss. On weekdays and evenings, you'll hear soft blues piped over the sound system. At the Sunday brunch, blues performances by regional acts are the norm. A Little Bit of Blues, a duo that is considered the house band, is fast becoming a local favorite. Their music runs the gamut from Delta blues to urban to R & B. While you're savoring the blues at Georgia Brown's, you'll find that the restaurant's menu more than lives up to Tifany's interior design. The chef, Cindy Wolf, intermingles traditional Southern recipes with nouvelle culinary techniques. The result is masterful. The chicken-fried steak, for example, is typical Southern fare, but you've got to try Wolf's version, served on a bed of fresh vegetables. Not all have found her experiments to their taste, however, and quite a bit of discussion occurred within the media about the propriety of Chef Wolf's undercooked, crunchy collards versus the more traditional, well-cooked ones. For those who prefer "down-home"-style greens, Georgia Brown's offers a choice. The menu also offers such dishes as smothered pork chops with sausage gravy, grilled Carolina black grouper, and cornmeal-crusted catfish escambiche. The peach-flavored iced tea is delicious. Whether it's for the Sunday Blues Brunch or just an afternoon interlude, this is *the* place where Washington comes together. Blue-collar workers and congressmen alike call Georgia Brown's their own.

KILIMANJARO

Location: 1724 California St. NW
Telephone: (202) 328-3839
Clientele: Young/Mature Adult
Format: Reggae/International
Calendar: Live Entertainment
Thurs.–Sun.; Dancing Tues.–Sun.
Cover/Minimum: Yes/No
Dress: Casual/Classy

Comments: Kilimanjaro primarily is a reggae and African dance club. Very popular among Washington's African and Caribbean populations, it also enjoys some success in the wider D.C. community. One room hosts small acts and a restaurant specializing in African and West Indian cuisine. Another room adjacent to the restaurant accommodates the larger acts. Kilimanjaro has featured international acts such as Jamaican singer Gregory Issacs, Nigerian singer Fela Kuti, and the late Zairian singer Franco.

165

KING OF FRANCE TAVERN

Location: 16 Church Circle (Annapolis, Md.)
Telephone: (301) 261-2206/(410) 269-0990
Clientele: Mature Adult
Format: Jazz
Calendar: Live Entertainment Fri.–Sun.
Cover/Minimum: Yes/No
Dress: Casual/Classy

Comments: The King of France Tavern is located in the Maryland Inn, one of the historic landmarks of Annapolis, Maryland. The inn dates back to the 18th century. High-backed hardwood chairs, tables fashioned from the tops of beer barrels, and cobblestone floors all combine to permeate the senses with an aura of history and tradition. Both the King of France Tavern and the Maryland Inn were restored to their original grandeur in the mid-1970s, when the current owners of the tavern transformed it into one of the area's premier jazz spots. This rectangular-shaped, low-lit room is tailor-made for the art. Charlie Byrd was the first act who performed here and has been a monthly staple since then. He consistently returns to rave reviews during breaks in his rigorous national and international touring schedule. Many of the legends of jazz stop by to jam when they're in the area. Dave Brubeck and the Count Basie Orchestra dropped in within days of each other during an October 1993 visit. You will definitely want to cruise over to Annapolis when you are visiting the Washington area. Tour the Naval Academy campus, visit the beautiful harbor, and by all means, cap off the evening with a session at the King of France Tavern. The room is somewhat small, with seating for about 100. Reservations are strongly encouraged.

LINCOLN THEATRE

Location: 1215 U St. NW
Telephone: (202) 328-6000
Clientele: Family/Young/Mature Adult
Format: Jazz/Blues/R & B/Stage Plays/
Musicals/Comedy
Calendar: Live Entertainment Varies
Cover/Minimum: Yes/na
Dress: Classy

Comments: The Lincoln Theatre reopened in February 1994 after a long absence from Washington's entertainment scene. The theater was founded in 1921 by Harry M. Crandall, the mogul of theater operators in Washington during that period. Abe Lichtman took over ownership in 1927, and during the "Roaring Twenties" and the following decade that witnessed the Harlem Renaissance, this was one of the premier entertainment showcases in the United States. The U Street area teemed with restaurants and cabarets where you could hear and see the likes of Pearl Bailey, Nat King Cole, and Billie Holiday. The Lincoln held many memorable performances by artists whose names are synonymous with the history of popular music in America: Louis Armstrong, Count Basie, Cab Calloway, Duke Ellington, Bessie Smith, and Fats Waller. When you visit the Lincoln today, you'll find it just as it was during the early 1920s. The restoration has spanned almost a decade, but the elegant end result was worth the wait. This 1,200-seat facility has beautiful box seats, ornate chandeliers, and bas-relief figures of President Lincoln on the walls just below the ceiling. The acoustics are outstanding, and there's not one obstructed view in the house. The lineup of stars who have already performed at the Lincoln since its grand opening signals a commitment to showcase the nation's top entertainers. Bobby "Blue" Bland, Cab Calloway, the Count Basie Orchestra, Sweet Honey in the Rock, and the Duke Ellington Orchestra led by Mercer Ellington are among the headliners thus far. Reservations are encouraged, especially for larger shows. The Lincoln Theatre is a good way to treat that special someone to a memorable evening as well as to a stroll through American history.

ONE STEP DOWN

Location: 2517 Pennsylvania Ave. NW
Telephone: (202) 331-8863
Clientele: Mature Adult
Format: Jazz
Calendar: Live Entertainment Thurs.–Mon.
Cover/Minimum: Yes/Yes (2 drinks)
Dress: Casual/Classy

Comments: One Step Down is an old establishment at the edge of Georgetown that has kept the faith and held true to its devotion to jazz. Joe Cohen opened the club in 1963. When he started, all he had to offer his patrons was a collection of jazz cuts on a jukebox. The jukebox is still here, and the cuts have grown into an enormous collection of jazz classics. As you walk in, you'll notice a rustic, dimly lit room that's small, but chock full of character and tradition. The collection of old "axes" (horns) hung along the walls adds to this feeling, as do the posters of jazz festivals long past. Seven booths line the right side of the room, and four long tables sit on the left, all hewn from rough oak. Remote jukebox stations sit atop the tables in each booth. It's difficult to imagine getting 75 people inside here, but make no mistake, this is definitely a jazz room! One Step Down began featuring live jazz about 18 years ago. Notables such as Ellis Marsalis, Curtis Fuller, Chet Baker, and Barry Harris have performed here. Often, jazz greats who are in town performing at larger venues will drop in for a jam session. The late, great Dizzy Gillespie would often come in just to shoot the breeze and relax. Dick Webster sometimes sends students from his Georgetown University jazz class here to do essays on the performers. Once a month, the University of Maryland does a jazz workshop here. The first set begins at 10:00 P.M. on weekends, followed by two more at 11:30 P.M. and 1:45 A.M. respectively. Get there by 8:30 P.M. for a seat because Cohen has a policy of not clearing the room before or between sets. Stop by and sample some jazz lore and one of the key ingredients in the Georgetown jazz tradition.

T. J. REMINGTON'S

Location: 1100 Wayne Ave. (Silver Spring, Md.)
Telephone: (301) 495-0080
Clientele: Young/Mature Adult
Format: Jazz
Calendar: Live Entertainment Wed.–Sat.
Cover/Minimum: Yes/No
Dress: Classy

Comments: T. J. Remington's is a sophisticated jazz room at the edge of Washington in Silver Spring, Maryland. What you get here is great ambience, superb jazz, and an outstanding continental menu. The dining room offers a panoramic view of downtown Silver Spring. The decor features burgundy tablecloths, polished hardwood, and brass rails throughout. Founded in 1985, T. J.'s has been featuring live jazz since 1990, when Emanuel Bailey, the club's booking agent, sold the owners on the idea of Silver Spring as an untapped jazz market. The first act was Spur of the Moment, a local fusion group lead by Wayne Bruce. That's how they got their name, in fact. Emanuel called Bruce, asked if he could put a group together to open T. J.'s jazz venue, and he did so, on the spur of the moment. The emphasis at T. J.'s is on hot, local jazz talent. The club is universally popular among Washington's growing population of jazz lovers who are under the age of 40-something. Stop in for a change of pace, a delicious meal, and a great evening of jazz.

TAKOMA STATION

Location: 6914 4th St. NW
Telephone: (202) 829-1999
Clientele: Mature/Young Adult
Format: Jazz
Calendar: Live Entertainment Nightly
Cover/Minimum: No/No
Dress: Casual/Classy

Comments: Takoma Station is on the Washington area's growing list of outstanding jazz supper clubs. It features great acoustics and an intimate environment for experiencing some hot, young, local jazz talent. Collaborations featuring vocalist Salina McDay is a regular act here. The photos of jazz legends adorning the walls give promise of a future that appears limitless for many of the gifted musicians who play at Takoma Station. While you're being entertained by the syncopated rhythms of jazz, you can enjoy a varied menu that includes crabcake platters, stuffed shrimp, fillet mignon, and the "Takoma Chill 'O'," a tasty and chunky chili concoction. Takoma Station was founded in 1984 and has enjoyed a growing following over the years. Visiting musicians often drop in to see what all the fuss is about: Stevie Wonder, the late Miles Davis, and Wynton Marsalis, to name a few. This is an establishment that you'll definitely want to visit when touring the Washington area.

TORNADO ALLEY

Location: 11319 Elkin St. (Wheaton, Md.)
Telephone: (301) 929-0795
Clientele: Young/Mature Adult
Format: Blues/R & B/Zydeco/Cajun/Rock & Roll/Country
Calendar: Live Entertainment Tues.–Sun.
Cover/Minimum: Yes/No
Dress: Casual/Classy

Comments: Tornado Alley is large and airy. Shades of blue dominate the room, from the blue-and-white checkerboard tiles and tablecloths to the blue formica-topped bar at the rear of the room. Tables are pulled together to form rows perpendicular to the stage. One wall in the back room displays coming attractions: promotion photos depicting some of the country's top blues stars. For May 1994, for example, the attractions included Billy Boy Arnold, Clarence "Gatemouth" Brown, Johnny Copeland, Clarence Carter, and Guitar Shorty. Another board shows upcoming zydeco and Cajun acts such as C. J. Chenier and Squeeze Bayou. Tornado Alley opens for dinner at 5:00 P.M. and serves a menu that features regional dishes such as "Louisiana Poor Boys," "Bayou State Etoufee," and red beans and rice. Other items include barbecue beef, pork, and chicken, and vegetarian specialties (collard greens, potato salad, and jalapeno corn muffins). The club's booking strategy is to feature top acts from a broad musical spectrum. Tornado Alley is one of the Washington area's premier places to hear the blues, so give them a call to find out what's on their calendar, or check the Friday entertainment section of the *Washington Post*.

TWINS

Location: 5516 Colorado Ave. NW
Telephone: (202) 882-2523
Clientele: Young/Mature Adult
Format: Jazz
Calendar: Live Entertainment
Wed.–Sun.
Cover/Minimum:
Yes (Fri.–Sat.)/Yes (2 drinks)
Dress: Casual/Classy

Comments: When Kelly Tesfaye was a student at the University of the District of Columbia, she helped pay her tuition by working part-time in various restaurants. She came to the conclusion that a jazz club could be both small and profitable, and so she and her sister Maze opened Twins in 1987. Theirs was a risk that has more than paid off. Twins is as intimate a hideaway as you'll find. On my first evening here, I had the pleasure of experiencing the sizzling piano virtuoso Kenny Drew. Performances at Twins are especially engaging because the room holds only 30 people at best. The seats are clustered about the stage in a manner that almost gives the sensation of hosting a concert in your own living room. Twins also offers a menu of Ethiopian, Haitian/Caribbean, and continental cuisine.

DINING

CHEF'S TABLE

Location: 4414 Benning Rd. NE
Telephone: (202) 398-6994
Proprietor: Albert Westbrook
Dress: Casual/Classy
Menu: Soul Food/Southern
Price: Modest
Hours: Tues.–Sat.: 5:00 P.M.–10:00 P.M.; Sun.: 2:00 P.M.–10:00 P.M.

Comments: When I visited Chef's Table for the first time, I was totally surprised. It may be one of Washington's best-kept secrets. From the moment you drive into their parking lot, you are aware that you're in for a special treat. This is simply one of the most attractive soul-food restaurants you'll find anywhere. The Chef's Table is best known for its all-you-can-eat soul-food buffet. I tried the potato salad, candied yams, pilaf gumbo, turkey gizzards, and cornbread muffins. All were excellent choices. The chitterlings, stuffed turkey rolls, and Southern fried chicken also were favorites among the patrons who continued to go back for more. Al Westbrook took over this establishment in 1972. His experience in the business goes back many years. When he was eight, he started working with his father, Clarence Westbrook, a man who opened his own first restaurant, Little Giant, during the Great Depression and went on to establish a chain of 13 restaurants in those economically challenging times. The elder Westbrook's restaurant on U Street was one of the largest in Washington during World War II, seating 150 people and catering to all the stars. In 1958, Clarence Westbrook opened Westbrook's, a full-service, 24-hour restaurant providing curbside service, take-out orders, and a sit-down menu. When Al took over from his ailing father in 1972, he renamed the restaurant Chef's Table. He also changed the format to a soul-food buffet and eliminated the 24-hour operations and the curbside service. Westbrook maintains that he has survived in this business because he never gives up and will spare no expense in keeping up the restaurant's appearance. A new generation of celebrities has been attracted to this second-generation establishment: the Reverend Jesse Jackson, Gladys Knight, and heavyweight champions Riddick Bowe and Evander Holyfield, to name a few. Don't miss the opportunity to dine at the Chef's Table when you're visiting the Washington area.

FACES

Location: 5625 Georgia Ave. NW
Telephone: (202) 291-6085
Proprietor: Donzell Tate
Dress: Casual/Classy
Menu: Soul Food
Price: Modest
Hours: Mon.–Thurs.: 11:30 A.M.–2:00 A.M.;
Fri.–Sat.: 6:00 P.M.–3:00 A.M.; Sun.: 4:00 P.M.–12:00 A.M.

Comments: Faces is one of Washington's oldest African American restaurants and lounges. The late Adolphus Williams founded the business in the early 1970s. Donzell Tate, one of the initial investors, became the principle owner in 1976. This attractive establishment has been a favorite meeting place for Washington's political, business, and educational leaders from its very inception. The decor is simple yet elegant in an understated way. The restaurant comfortably seats about 100 patrons. The fried chicken and fried fish are the entrees that most patrons rave about when speaking of the restaurant. According to Tate, Faces has used the same secret ingredients for more than 20 years to create a batter that renders the fish and chicken crisp, yet moist and tender. You'll especially want to try the mouth-watering fillet of trout. Turkey, ham, and collards are delivered fresh from the market and cooked daily on the premises. So are their homemade sweet-potato pies and the macaroni and cheese, also favorites among the long list of satisfied patrons. Other menu items include calf's liver and onions, a crabcake platter, barbecue ribs, and an array of fried fish such as catfish, trout, and whiting. Chitterlings are served on occasion. The restaurant has two kitchens. In one, you'll find Chef Tate busily preparing the entrees, while in the other, Chef Eloise Booker, who has been with the restaurant for 18 years, works magic with the sweet-potato pie, collards, and macaroni and cheese. Faces has been described by some as one of Washington's defining institutions. On weekends, or whenever patrons are in a festive mood, a few of the tables are moved aside to accommodate a dance floor. Stop by Faces when you're in the Washington area for a great meal and an opportunity to experience the pulse of D.C.

FLORIDA AVENUE GRILL

Location: 1100 Florida Ave. NW
Telephone: (202) 265-1586
Proprietor: Lacey C. Wilson
Dress: Casual
Menu: Soul Food
Price: Very Modest
Hours: Tues.–Sat.: 6:00 A.M.–9:00 P.M.

Comments: Mr. and Mrs. Lacey Wilson, Sr., came to Washington by way of Burlington, North Carolina. They founded the Florida Avenue Grill in 1944. They staked their reputation on good food and fast service, qualities which especially endeared the Wilson restaurant to its primary clientele at the time, D.C. taxi drivers. Lacey Wilson, Jr., took over the family business in 1974. The Florida Avenue Grill now has expanded its base of loyal patrons to national proportions. The longevity of this landmark institution is a testament to the quality of service provided here. Located about two blocks from Howard University, it is the flagship of Washington's soul-food establishments. How popular is this restaurant? When you walk in, take a look at the autographed photos above the counter. Clint Eastwood, Natalie Cole, the Reverend Joseph Lowery, and professional basketball star Charles Barkley are but a few of the luminaries who have found their way to this modest, but splendid restaurant. This is down-home cooking in the middle of the nation's capital. I feasted on a bountiful portion of liver and onions, collard greens, and rice. Other items from the menu include barbecue beef, smothered pork chops, chitterlings, ham hocks, and fillet of fresh fried fish. Homemade desserts include bread pudding and peach cobbler. You'll also find the Florida Avenue Grill an excellent choice for breakfast. Try the "Chef's Special" featuring "country ham n' eggs, red eye gravy, grits, fried apples or home fries, hot biscuit and coffee." Applauded by *Washingtonian* magazine as a perennial "best cheap eat," this is one Washington monument you can't leave the city without visiting.

FRENCH'S

Location: 1365 H St. NE
Telephone: (202) 396-0991/0992
Proprietor: The French Family
Dress: Casual/Classy
Menu: Soul Food
Price: Modest
Hours: Mon.–Sat.: 8:00 A.M.–9:00 P.M.; Sun.: 8:00 A.M.–6:00 P.M.

Comments: French's is a highly regarded soul-food restaurant located in Northeast Washington. It is both spacious and attractive. You can tell volumes about an establishment by what is placed along its walls. In this case, photographs of numerous celebrities and renowned public figures pay tribute to the quality of the soul-food fare that you'll enjoy here. Some who have found their way to French's include Representative Maxine Waters, D.C. Mayor Sharon Pratt Kelly, the Jackson Southernaires, and the Jacksons. The walls are also lined with testaments to the public and community service for which John French and his daughter Sharon are well known. One photo shows John French being presented with a White House Presidential Award for his work with the D.C. Private Enterprise Council's 1984 Summer Jobs Program. Moving through the serving line, you will come upon a delicious array of soulful choices. The fare includes items such as bread pudding, barbecue ribs, baked fish, chitterlings, black-eyed peas, and rice. I was delighted with my choice of baked beef ribs, collard greens, snap beans, and a cornbread muffin. The French family has been in the restaurant business for almost two decades. They relocated their restaurant to the Northeast section of the city in 1987 to help fuel a revitalization of the neighborhood. Their flagship enterprise is a model for any similar efforts throughout the United States.

JOPLIN'S

Location: 2225 Georgia Ave. NW
Telephone: (202) 462-5400
Proprietor: Howard University
Dress: Casual/Classy
Menu: Soul Food/Continental
Price: Moderate
Hours: Daily: Breakfast:
7:00 A.M.–11:30 A.M.;
Lunch: 11:30 A.M.–2:00 P.M.; Dinner: 5:00 P.M.–10:00 P.M.

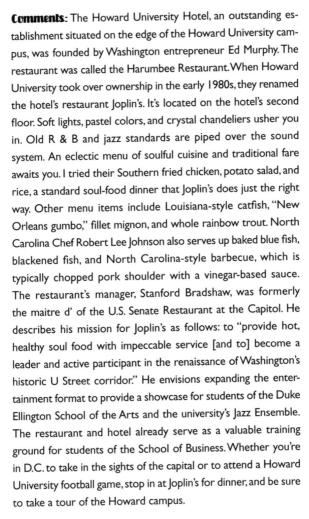

Comments: The Howard University Hotel, an outstanding establishment situated on the edge of the Howard University campus, was founded by Washington entrepreneur Ed Murphy. The restaurant was called the Harumbee Restaurant. When Howard University took over ownership in the early 1980s, they renamed the hotel's restaurant Joplin's. It's located on the hotel's second floor. Soft lights, pastel colors, and crystal chandeliers usher you in. Old R & B and jazz standards are piped over the sound system. An eclectic menu of soulful cuisine and traditional fare awaits you. I tried their Southern fried chicken, potato salad, and rice, a standard soul-food dinner that Joplin's does just the right way. Other menu items include Louisiana-style catfish, "New Orleans gumbo," fillet mignon, and whole rainbow trout. North Carolina Chef Robert Lee Johnson also serves up baked blue fish, blackened fish, and North Carolina-style barbecue, which is typically chopped pork shoulder with a vinegar-based sauce. The restaurant's manager, Stanford Bradshaw, was formerly the maitre d' of the U.S. Senate Restaurant at the Capitol. He describes his mission for Joplin's as follows: to "provide hot, healthy soul food with impeccable service [and to] become a leader and active participant in the renaissance of Washington's historic U Street corridor." He envisions expanding the entertainment format to provide a showcase for students of the Duke Ellington School of the Arts and the university's Jazz Ensemble. The restaurant and hotel already serve as a valuable training ground for students of the School of Business. Whether you're in D.C. to take in the sights of the capital or to attend a Howard University football game, stop in at Joplin's for dinner, and be sure to take a tour of the Howard campus.

177

LEVI'S NORTH CAROLINA BARBECUE

Location: 5310 Indianhead Hwy. (Fort Washington, Md.)
Telephone: (301) 567-1700
Proprietor: Levi and Gloria Durham
Dress: Casual/Classy
Menu: Soul Food/Continental
Price: Modest
Hours: Mon.–Thurs.:
11:00 A.M.–10:00 P.M.;
Fri.–Sat.: 11:00 A.M.–11:00 P.M.

Comments: Levi and Gloria Durham are originally from Goldsboro, North Carolina, and they've brought a little bit of the Carolinas to Washington by way of their soul-food restaurant. Levi Durham's first taste of entrepreneurship came at the age of 20 when he owned and operated a gas station; he and Gloria ventured into the restaurant business in 1989. Levi's has a large and faithful following, and you're best advised to call ahead and place your order so that you won't have to wait in line. The restaurant has developed quite a reputation, so much so that Senator Ted Kennedy invites Levi Durham out to do the ribs at his annual Fourth of July barbecue. Levi's also caters most of Riddick Bowe's parties. While Durham's first restaurant is better suited to take-out orders, his second restaurant, opened in November 1993 at 1233 Brentwood Road NE, is spacious enough to accommodate Levi's many appreciative customers in the D.C. area. Both restaurants offer a tantalizing menu that features baked fish, fried fish, North Carolina barbecue ribs, soulful veggies, and sweet pies. My favorite was the fried fish with potato salad and hushpuppies. The North Carolina barbecue is also a treat. Levi Durham credits the popularity of the ribs to a special vinegar-based sauce developed by Montel Scott, Sr., of Goldsboro, North Carolina, and to slow-cooked meat that is prepared fresh daily. When asked about the key to his success, Levi told me, "We open each day at the restaurant with all the employees holding hands in a circle and offering a prayer of thanks." Take a tip from the locals: include Levi's among your dining choices when you visit the nation's capital.

MA'S PLACE

Location: 6912 4th St. NW
Telephone: (202) 723-4551
Proprietor: Mary Morgan
Dress: Casual/Classy
Menu: Soul Food/Southern
Price: Modest
Hours: Tues.–Fri.: 11:30 A.M.–9:00 P.M.;
Sat.–Sun.: 2:00 P.M.–9:00 P.M.

Comments: Ma's Place is located right next to the popular jazz club, Takoma Station. Ma's has the atmosphere of a European cafe, with its green tabletops, flower vases, and soft jazz piped in over the sound system. The restaurant has seating for 35 to 40 patrons, and what you get when you sit down for a meal there is like grandmother's cooking served up in the living room the old-fashioned way, with a smile and loads of conversation. The menu includes "oven-fried chicken (chicken baked in Ma's herbs & spices)," "Bar-B-que chicken (oven-baked and bar-b-qued with cousin Artie's secret sauce)," smothered pork chops, turkey with onions, and "Ma's Veggies" (collard greens, cabbage, and string beans). There's also Ma's famous cornbread dressing, made from a recipe taught to her by her grandmother. The vegetables are hot and spicy but cooked without meats, a fact that is appreciated by a large number of vegetarian patrons. You must try Ma's homemade apple and sweet-potato pie as well. Ma is Mary Morgan, a retired D.C. schoolteacher who started the business with her children, Beverly, Brenda, Elizabeth, Judith, Terry, and Tony, in August 1992. All of the Morgans are active in making the restuarant a go. Cousins Artie and Michael Hazels also lend a helping hand. The inspiration for this venture was the accomplishments of Mary's late father, Eugene James, who ran the White House kitchen under the Coolidge administration and also operated a catering business in the late 1940s. The Morgans' entrepreneurial dream has been realized in grand fashion. Singers Jennifer Holliday and Nancy Wilson and the Reverend Jesse Jackson are among the celebrities who have made their way here. Don't miss the opportunity to experience the hospitality and down-home cuisine at Ma's Place.

SOUTHERN DINER

Location: 6577 Coventry Way (Clinton, Md.)

Telephone: (301) 868-0815

Proprietor: John Kelly, Sr. and Willie Holt

Dress: Casual

Menu: Soul Food

Price: Modest

Hours: Mon.–Thurs.: 7:00 A.M.–9:00 P.M.;
Fri.: 7:00 A.M.–10:00 P.M.; Sat.: 8:00 A.M.–10:00 P.M.;
Sun.: 8:00 A.M.–8:00 P.M.

Comments: John Kelly, Sr., and Willie Holt established the Southern Diner in 1990. Kelly had owned an auto body shop for a number of years, and Holt had served as head chef in various Washington-area restaurants for more than 40 years. The friends pooled their capital and expertise to found this excellent soul-food eatery. Both their success and the quality of their food have been praised by the *Washington Post* and *Washingtonian* magazine. Riddick Bowe is a regular customer. Gerald Levert and Luther Vandross have stopped by. Kelly's son John Junior and daughter Linda both help out to make this restaurant a family affair. The menu features a variety of soulful dishes such as chopped, North Carolina beef barbecue, Cajun catfish, chicken and dumplings, chitterlings, stewed tomatoes, and baby lima beans. I was very pleased with the fillet of whiting, string beans, and red beans and rice. To get to the Southern Diner from downtown D.C., take the 495 Beltway north to exit 7A (Branch Avenue), proceed through three traffic signals, and turn left at Coventry Way. The diner is on the left as you pass the Riggs Bank. It's a 15-minute ride from downtown that's well worth the trip.

DANCING

ECLIPSE

Location: 2820 Bladensburg Rd. NE

Telephone: (202) 526-3533

Clientele: Mature Adult

Format: R & B

Calendar: Dancing Nightly; Live Entertainment Quarterly

Cover/Minimum: Yes/No

Dress: Classy

Comments: "They're hand-dancing down in Northeast." That's how Eclipse was first described to me. The club and its venue are a throwback to days long gone. When I walked in, I was reminded of my youth: beautiful summer days in the late 1960s when everyone down in South Louisiana was "swinging out" to the tunes of the Drifters, Sam and Dave, and Aretha Franklin. That's what you get when you enter the Eclipse. It's a beautifully manicured, spacious lounge that easily accommodates 299. The dance floor is the focal point. The bar faces one side of the dance floor, the deejay booth faces the other, and rows of tables overlook vast expanse of, again, "the floor." The deejay spins a mood that transports you back in time while the dancers, appreciative all, glide across the floor. Some of the top R & B acts that have performed at the Eclipse include Bobby "Blue" Bland, the Impressions, the Main Ingredient, and the Manhattans. When I think of this club, the words to a song immortalized by the late Sam Cooke come to mind: "They're having a party, everbody's swinging; dancing to the music." I spent a wonderful evening here, and you will too!

181

CLUB ZEI

Location: 1412 I St. NW
Telephone: (202) 842-2445
Clientele: Young/Mature Adult
Format: Commercial/House/Techno
Calendar: Live Entertainment Monthly; Dancing Wed.–Sat.
Cover/Minimum: Yes/No
Dress: Classy

Comments: Club Zei is one of Washington's newest and trendiest dance spots. When I called to get a description of the club, assistant manager Eton Thomas told me that its clientele resembled the United Nations. That turned out to be fairly accurate. Club Zei draws its patrons primarily from Washington's hip local and international set. It's also a favorite among visiting celebrities, professional athletes, and the political (bipartisan!) crowd. Shanice Williams, an R & B star, Georgie Porgie, a Chicago house star, and Kellee, another house star, are some of the acts that have performed. The club has the latest in laser lights and sound systems, features three levels, and is a constant party. The room holds 850. If you're interested in experiencing the best D.C. has to offer in the way of high-tech amenities and high-energy dancing, Club Zei is an excellent choice.

PIER 7

Location: 650 Water St. NW
Telephone: (202) 554-2500
Clientele: Young/Mature Adult
Format: R & B/Jazz
Calendar: Live Entertainment & Dancing Tues.–Sat.
Cover/Minimum: No/Yes (1 drink)
Dress: Classy

Comments: Pier 7 was founded in 1972, and it has always had a jazz venue that features a house band. Since 1987, Elite, a classical jazz trio, has been the band of choice. The name of this establishment gives a hint of what you'll find here. It's a waterfront hideaway that has long been popular among D.C. power brokers. While the band is well versed in the classical jazz idiom, what the customers seem to prefer is the opportunity to dance to R & B oldies.

RITZ NIGHTCLUB

Location: 919 E St. NW
Telephone: (202) 638-2582
Clientele: Young/Mature Adult
Format: Top 40/House/Reggae/Jazz
Calendar: Live Entertainment Varies; Dancing Wed., Fri.–Sun.
Cover/Minimum: Yes/No
Dress: Classy

Comments: The Ritz is one of Washington's most exciting and popular entertainment phenomenons. A spacious and attractive four-story club, the Ritz offers something for everyone. The first floor features live jazz in one room, house music in another. Go upstairs, and you'll find reggae on one floor and oldies on yet another. While you might think that these contrasting venues are a bit much under one roof, you have only to look at the enormous popularity of the Ritz to see that the idea works. Judging by the number of celebrities such as Angela Bofield, Michael Jordan, and Eddie Murphy who have visited, the Ritz is increasingly gaining national renown as well. The club features local artists playing a range of jazz from straightahead to modern each Friday and Saturday night. Reggae Night is a regular feature each Wednesday, and Sunday nights have traditionally been a big draw for college students. Will Downing, Aaron Hall, Chick Corea, and Diane Reeves are among the national acts that have been booked here. Advanced sales are conducted for the larger shows. The club also hosts numerous private parties such as fundraisers for political campaigns and a recent event for the Congressional Black Caucus. This is an outstanding way to spend an evening while visiting the Washington area.